The New Ninja
Dual Zone
Air Fryer Cookbook

1600 Days Fast & Fresh and Delicious Ninja Foodi Recipes for
Beginners and Busy people incl. Dinners, Sides, Snacks, Lunches & More

Dale P. Rodriguez

Contents

CHAPTER 3 FAMILY FAVOURITES (BRITISH CLASSICS) 21

CHAPTER 4 POULTRY 28

CHAPTER 5 FISH & SEAFOOD 35

CHAPTER 6 BEEF, PORK & LAMB

CHAPTER 7 SNACKS & APPETIZERS

INTRODUCTION

Welcome to the UK Ninja Dual Zone Air Fryer Cookbook! As a passionate food lover and a proud owner of the Ninja Dual Zone Air Fryer, I couldn't be more excited to share this collection of delicious and versatile recipes with you. Whether you're a seasoned cook or just starting your culinary journey, this cookbook is designed to help you make the most out of your air fryer and take your cooking skills to new heights.

Air frying is a cooking method that has gained popularity in recent years and has been hailed as a healthier alternative to traditional frying. It involves using hot air circulated at high speed to cook food, resulting in a crispy exterior similar to deep frying but with significantly less oil. Its popularity is evident through the variety of air fryer models available on the market, ranging from compact countertop appliances to built-in oven designs. As technology continues to advance, we can expect further refinements and innovations in air frying, making it an increasingly integral part of modern cooking. Air frying can be used to cook a wide variety of foods, including chips, chicken wings, vegetables, fish, and even desserts like doughnuts. It allows you to achieve a crispy texture and golden brown colour without the excessive oiliness associated with deep frying. However, it's important to note that air frying may not produce the same results as deep frying in terms of taste and texture, but it offers a healthier alternative that many people find satisfying.

In this cookbook, we will explore the UK Ninja Dual Zone Air Fryer, a versatile kitchen appliance designed to revolutionize your cooking experience. This state-of-the-art air fryer boasts an array of features that make it stand out from other models on the market! The UK Ninja Dual Zone Air Fryer combines versatility, convenience, and cutting-edge dual-zone technology to elevate your cooking endeavours. With its ability to cook two different foods simultaneously, its wide range of cooking methods, and its user-friendly controls, this air fryer is a must-have for any kitchen enthusiast seeking to create delicious and healthy meals with ease! Throughout the pages of this recipe collection, you'll find a diverse range of recipes, carefully crafted to cater to different tastes and dietary preferences. Whether you're looking for indulgent comfort food, healthy vegan options, or air fryer staples for busy weeknights, there's something for everyone. Each recipe is accompanied by a detailed list of the ingredients, step-by-step instructions, and helpful tips to guide you every step of the way. Join me on this culinary adventure as we explore the endless possibilities of the UK Ninja Dual Zone Air Fryer. Let's unleash our creativity, elevate our cooking skills, and create delicious meals that will impress family and friends!

Mastering the Art of Air Frying with the UK Ninja Dual Zone Air Fryer

Picture this: savouring crispy, golden-brown fries or juicy chicken wings without the guilt. Air frying offers a healthier alternative to traditional deep-frying methods. By utilizing hot air instead of copious amounts of oil, air fryers can significantly

reduce the fat content of your favourite dishes, making them more waistline-friendly. One of the most enticing aspects of air frying is the ability to achieve that desirable crispy texture without the hassle. Air fryers employ a technology that evenly distributes heat, resulting in a delightful crunch on the outside, while keeping the inside moist and tender. Say goodbye to soggy fried foods forever! Did you know that air frying has become a global sensation and is rapidly gaining popularity among food enthusiasts? In the blink of an eye, air frying has become more than just a trend; it's revolutionizing the way we cook and enjoy our favourite dishes! Let's explore its major advantages!

The Ninja Dual Zone Air Fryer has a 7.6L capacity that feeds up to 8 people. It has six cooking functions: Max Crisp, Air Fry, Bake, Roast, Dehydrate, and Reheat. It is up to 75% faster than fan ovens and up to 75% less fat than traditional frying methods. The appliance is easy to clean with dishwasher-safe parts1. The appliance has two individual baskets which are 3.8 L each2. The UK Ninja Dual Zone Air Fryer features user-friendly controls that make operation effortless. It has a selection of pre-set cooking programs for popular dishes, making it convenient for beginners or those who prefer quick and hassle-free cooking. Additionally, customizable cooking settings allow you to tailor the cooking process to your specific preferences. The appliance offers precise temperature control, allowing you to set the cooking temperature ranging from 40°C to 240°C for optimal cooking results. The digital display provides clear and easy-to-read information, making it simple to adjust and monitor the cooking process. The UK Ninja Dual Zone Air Fryer has two crisper plates that can be used in place of the cooking baskets; these plates are designed to provide a crispy texture to your food! And last but not least, there is a drip tray that is designed to collect any excess oil or grease that drips from your food during cooking. Lovely!

According to TechRadar, the Ninja Foodi Dual Zone Air Fryer is one of the best air fryers in 2023. It combines innovative technology, convenient features, and a generous capacity to deliver efficient and delicious cooking results. It offers versatility, precision, and ease of use, making it an excellent addition to any kitchen. So, why we should have Ninja Dual Zone Air Fryer?

- **Unique technology.** One of the key highlights of the UK Ninja Dual Zone Air Fryer is its unique dual-zone technology. Unlike conventional air fryers that typically have a single cooking zone, this appliance is equipped with two independent cooking zones. Each zone can be individually controlled, allowing you to simultaneously cook different foods at different temperatures and durations. This means you can prepare a main course and a side dish simultaneously, optimizing your cooking time and ensuring that both items are cooked to perfection. And best of all – each zone has its own temperature and cooking time controls, providing flexibility and efficiency in meal preparation.

- **Versatility.** The UK Ninja Dual Zone Air Fryer is not limited to just frying. These incredible appliances can grill, roast, bake, and even dehydrate various foods. From perfectly cooked steaks to tender roasted vegetables, air fryers can handle a wide range of culinary creations, making them a versatile addition to any kitchen. With its wide temperature range and multiple pre-set cooking functions, you have the freedom to experiment with various recipes and culinary techniques. Whether you want to enjoy crispy chips, succulent chicken wings, mouthwatering pastries, or even homemade dried fruits, the UK Ninja Dual Zone Air Fryer has got you covered!

- **Convenience.** The appliance features a user-friendly control panel with a digital display, making it effortless to adjust the temperature, cooking time, and cooking zones. It also offers convenient preset functions for popular dishes, simplifying the cooking process even further. Additionally, the UK Ninja Dual Zone Air Fryer is equipped with a spacious cooking basket and a generous capacity, allowing you to cook larger portions and cater to your family or guests with ease. With its generous capacity that can accommodate up to 5.2 litres of food, this machine is perfect for cooking meals for the entire family or a gathering of friends. The spacious cooking basket ensures you can prepare a variety of dishes in one go!

- **Time and energy-saving technology.** With our fast-paced lifestyles, finding efficient cooking methods is a game-changer! the UK Ninja Dual Zone Air Fryer delivers on this front by significantly reducing cooking times. By circulating hot air at high speeds, it can cook food faster than conventional methods, cutting down on the time spent in the kitchen and leaving you more time to enjoy your meal. As we become more environmentally conscious, air frying offers a greener way to cook. Compared to conventional ovens, the UK Ninja Dual Zone Air Fryer requires less energy to operate, making it an eco-friendly choice. So, not only can you enjoy delicious meals, but you can also reduce your carbon footprint in the process. Lovely!

- **Safety features.** And last but not least, the UK Ninja Dual Zone Air Fryer is designed with safety and convenience in mind. It has a non-stick coating on the cooking basket, which facilitates easy cleaning and prevents food from sticking. The appliance also has built-in safety features such as overheat protection and an automatic shut-off function, ensuring that your cooking experience is safe and worry-free! The cool-touch handle and exterior prevent accidental burns, making it safe to handle during and after cooking.

How to Clean the Ninja Dual Zone Air Fryer?

To clean your Ninja Dual Zone Air Fryer, follow these steps:

- Unplug the air fryer: Make sure the unit is unplugged from the power source before cleaning to ensure safety.
- Let the appliance cool down for at least 30 minutes before starting the cleaning process. The air fryer becomes hot during cooking, and cleaning it immediately can be dangerous.
- Take out all removable accessories from the air fryer. This typically includes the cooking basket, crisper plate, and any other detachable parts.
- Wash the removable parts with warm water and a mild dishwashing detergent. Use a non-abrasive sponge or cloth to gently scrub away any food residue. Rinse thoroughly and allow the parts to dry completely before reassembling.
- Use a damp cloth or sponge to wipe down the interior and exterior surfaces of the air fryer. Avoid using abrasive cleaners or scouring pads, as they can scratch the finish. If there are stubborn stains, you can mix a small amount

of baking soda with water to create a paste and gently scrub the affected areas. Wipe off any residue with a clean, damp cloth.

- Use a soft brush or cloth to clean the heating element. Be careful not to damage it while cleaning. Remove any debris or grease buildup that may have accumulated.
- Wipe the control panel with a damp cloth, ensuring that no liquid enters the control panel area. If there are tough stains, use a mild dishwashing detergent and a soft cloth to gently clean them.
- Once all the components are dry, reassemble the air fryer by placing the cleaned accessories back into their respective positions.
- After cleaning, make sure your Ninja Dual Zone Air Fryer is completely dry before storing it. Store it in a cool, dry place where it is protected from moisture and dust.

Potential Risks and Concerns

- **Burn Risks.** The air fryer utilizes hot air to cook food, and as a result, the exterior of the appliance can become very hot during operation. There is a risk of burns if you accidentally touch hot surfaces, such as the exterior or the frying basket. It's important to use oven mitts or other protective gear when handling the appliance.
- **Oil and Grease Splatter.** When cooking certain types of food, particularly those with high-fat content, there is a possibility of oil or grease splattering. This can occur when opening the cooking basket or when adding or removing food. To minimize the risk of burns or other injuries, it's advisable to handle the food carefully and use protective gear if necessary.
- **Electrical Hazards.** Like any electrical appliance, there is a potential risk of electrical hazards if the unit is not used or maintained properly. Make sure to read and follow the manufacturer's instructions, avoid overloading electrical circuits, and never immerse the appliance in water or use it near water sources.
- **Food Overcooking or Burning.** Air fryers work

by circulating hot air around the food to cook it. If the cooking time or temperature is not properly adjusted, there is a risk of food becoming overcooked or burned. It's important to carefully follow the recommended cooking instructions for different types of food and monitor the cooking process to ensure optimal results.

Tips and Tricks for the Ninja Dual Zone Air Fryer

- Just like with a traditional oven, preheating the air fryer can help ensure even cooking
- and crispy results. Follow the manufacturer's instructions for preheating your Ninja Dual Zone Air Fryer before adding your food.
- For optimal air circulation and even cooking, arrange your food in a single layer inside the cooking basket. Overcrowding the basket can result in unevenly cooked food.
- During the cooking process, consider shaking the basket or flipping the food halfway through to ensure even browning. This helps to achieve a crispy texture on all sides.
- Cooking times and temperatures may vary depending on the recipe and the quantity of food. Start with the recommended settings in your recipe, but don't be afraid to adjust them to achieve your desired results. Keep an eye on the food and make adjustments as needed.
- The Ninja Dual Zone Air Fryer is not limited to just fish and chips. Experiment with a variety of foods like vegetables, seafood, meats, and even desserts. This can be a great tool for healthier cooking options.
- If you're concerned about food sticking to the basket, consider using parchment paper or aluminium foil. Cut them to fit the basket and place them at the bottom before adding the food. This can make cleanup easier and prevent sticking.
- Pre-treat foods for extra crispiness. To achieve an extra crispy texture, you can pre-treat certain foods. For example, lightly coat vegetables with a small amount of oil or toss chicken wings in a mixture of cornstarch and spices before air

frying. These steps can enhance the crispiness of the end result.

To sum up, let's answer frequently asked questions about Ninja Foodi Dual Zone.

1. What is the Ninja Foodi Dual Zone?

The Ninja Foodi Dual Zone is a kitchen appliance that combines several cooking methods in one unit, allowing you to cook multiple dishes simultaneously.

2. What are the key features of the Ninja Foodi Dual Zone?

The Ninja Foodi Dual Zone features two independent cooking zones, multiple cooking functions, and a large capacity for versatile cooking.

3. Can I use the Ninja Foodi Dual Zone as a regular oven?

Yes, the Ninja Foodi Dual Zone functions as a regular oven, allowing you to cook meals faster and retain more nutrients compared to conventional cooking methods.

4. How does the air frying function work in the Ninja Foodi Dual Zone?

The air frying function in the Ninja Foodi Dual Zone uses super-hot air to give your food a crispy and golden texture without the need for excessive oil.

5. Is the Ninja Foodi Dual Zone easy to clean?

Yes, the Ninja Foodi Dual Zone is designed for easy cleaning. The cooking basket, crisper plates, and other accessories are dishwasher-safe.

6. Can I adjust the cooking time and temperature for each zone separately?

Absolutely! The Ninja Foodi Dual Zone allows you to independently control the time and temperature for each cooking zone, enabling you to cook different dishes simultaneously.

7. What is Dual Zone technology in the Ninja Foodi Dual Zone?

The Dual Zone technology in the Ninja Foodi Dual Zone refers to its ability to create two separate cooking zones within the same appliance. This feature is typically found in Ninja's air fryers.

8. What is the capacity of the Ninja Foodi Dual Zone?

The Ninja Foodi Dual Zone has a generous capacity, typically allowing you to cook up to 6 quarts of food in each cooking zone.

9. Can I dehydrate food with the Ninja Foodi Dual Zone?

Yes, the Ninja Foodi Dual Zone comes with a dehydrating function, which allows you to preserve fruits, vegetables, and more.

10. Is the Ninja Foodi Dual Zone safe to use?

Yes, the Ninja Foodi Dual Zone is designed with safety in mind! It includes various safety features, and, like any electrical appliance, it should be safe to use as long as you follow the manufacturer's instructions and safety guidelines.

On that note, let's dive in and make every meal a culinary masterpiece!

CHAPTER 1 BREAKFAST

Classic Sausages with Eggs

Prep time: 5 minutes / Cook time: 16 minutes / Serves 4

Ingredients

- 4 sausage links, raw and uncooked
- 4 eggs, uncooked
- 2 tablespoons milk
- Sea salt and ground black pepper, to taste
- 4 cherry tomatoes, halved

Instructions

1. Pierce the sausages all over using a sharp knife to help release more fat.
2. Now, add sausages to the zone 1 drawer.
3. Take a jug and whisk the eggs and milk in it. Then, season the egg mixture with salt and black pepper.
4. Spoon the egg mixture into lightly greased muffin cases; top them with tomatoes and add them to the zone 2 drawer.
5. Select zone 1 and pair it with . Select zone 2 and pair it with "AIR FRY" at 180°C for 9 minutes
6. Select "SYNC" followed by the "START/STOP" button. At the halfway point, turn the sausages over with silicone-tipped tongs to promote even cooking.
7. Bon appétit!

Baked Avocado Eggs

Prep time: 10 minutes / Cook time: 10 minutes / Serves 6

Ingredients

- 3 large avocados, pitted and cut in half
- 6 small eggs
- Garlic salt and cayenne pepper, to taste
- 100g cooked bacon, crumbled
- 35g parmesan cheese, crumbled
- 2 tbsp lemon juice
- 1/2 tsp garlic granules
- 1 tbsp yellow mustard

Instructions

1. Cut the avocados in half and carefully remove the pits.
2. Scoop out 1-2 tablespoons of avocado flesh from the centre of each half; reserve.
3. Crack an egg into each avocado cup. Season with garlic salt and cayenne pepper to taste. Top with bacon and add avocado halves to both drawers.
4. Select zone 1 and pair it with "BAKE" at 190°C for 10 minutes. Select "MATCH" followed by the "START/STOP" button.
5. At the halfway point, top avocado eggs with parmesan cheese. Reinsert drawers to resume cooking.
6. In the meantime, whisk the remaining avocado flesh with lemon juice, garlic granules, and yellow mustard.
7. Drizzle the sauce over the top of the avocado eggs.
8. Bon appétit!

Grandma's Breakfast Casserole

Prep time: 10 minutes / Cook time: 15 minutes / Serves 6

Ingredients

- 300g beef sausage, crumbled
- 1 medium shallot, thinly sliced
- 1 green bell pepper, seeded and diced
- 250g chestnut mushrooms, sliced
- 8 large eggs, beaten
- 100ml whole milk
- 125g cheddar cheese, grated
- Garlic salt and ground black pepper, to taste

Instructions

1. Add all the Ingredients to a mixing bowl and stir until everything is well combined.
2. Spoon the mixture into two lightly-greased baking tins. Add the baking tins to the drawers.
3. Select zone 1 and pair it with "BAKE" at 190°C for 15 minutes. Select "MATCH" followed by the "START/STOP" button.
4. At the halfway point, gently stir the Ingredients with a spoon. Reinsert drawers to resume cooking.
5. Bon appétit!

Protein Flapjacks

Prep time: 10 minutes / Cook time: 20 minutes / Serves 8-10

Ingredients

- 300g old-fashioned rolled oats
- 100g acacia (or clear) honey
- 2 tbsp chia seeds
- 2 tbsp almonds, chopped

- 200g peanut butter
- A pinch of sea salt
- A pinch of grated nutmeg
- 1/2 tsp cinnamon powder

Instructions

1. Start by preheating your Ninja Dual Zone Air Fryer to 175°C. Now, brush two baking tins with nonstick cooking spray.
2. In your processor, mix the rolled oats, honey, chia seeds, almonds, peanut butter, salt, nutmeg, and cinnamon.
3. Divide the batter between the prepared baking tins. Lower the baking tins into the drawers.
4. Select zone 1 and pair it with "BAKE" at 180°C for 20 minutes. Select "MATCH" followed by the "START/STOP" button.
5. Allow your flapjacks to cool for about 10 minutes before slicing them into bars or squares.
6. Bon appétit!

Cinnamon Apple Muffins

Prep time: 10 minutes / Cook time: 15 minutes / Serves 8

Ingredients

- 2 small eggs
- 100ml pot natural low-fat yoghurt
- 2 medium apples, cored, peeled and grated
- 4 tbsp clear honey
- 100g butter, melted
- 1/2 tsp vanilla extract
- 150g self-raising flour
- 50g rolled oats, plus extra for sprinkling
- 1 tbsp flaxseed meal
- A pinch of sea salt
- 1 tsp ground cinnamon
- 1/2 tsp grated nutmeg, preferably freshly grated
- 100g brown sugar

Instructions

1. Remove a crisper plate from your Ninja Dual Zone Air Fryer and preheat the machine to 160°C for 5 minutes. Lightly butter the inside of 8 muffin cases.
2. In a jug, thoroughly combine all the liquid ingredients. Tip the remaining (or dry) ingredients, except the apples, into a separate mixing bowl, and mix to combine.
3. Slowly and gradually, add the dry Ingredients to the wet ingredients; fold in the apples and mix to combine.
4. (Do not overmix as this will make your muffins heavy).

5. Scrape the batter into the prepared muffin cases. Divide the muffin cases between drawers.
6. Select zone 1 and pair it with "BAKE" at 160°C for 15 minutes. Select "MATCH" followed by the "START/STOP" button.
7. Using a toothpick, check your muffins for doneness; transfer them to a wire rack and leave to cool.
8. Store your muffins in a sealed container for up to 3 days. Enjoy!

British-Style Bacon and Eggs

Prep time: 5 minutes / Cook time: 12 minutes / Serves 5

Ingredients

- 5 rashers smoked bacon
- 5 large eggs
- Sea salt and ground black pepper, to taste
- 100g canned white beans, drained and rinsed

Instructions

1. Insert a crisper plate in the zone 1 drawer. Spray the plate with nonstick cooking oil. Crack the eggs in lightly greased muffin cases and season them with salt and pepper.
2. Add smoked bacon to the zone 1 drawer; add the muffin cases to the zone 2 drawer.
3. Select zone 1 and pair it with "AIR FRY" at 180°C for 12 minutes. Select zone 2 and pair it with "AIR FRY" at 180°C for 9 minutes
4. Select "SYNC" followed by the "START/STOP" button. At the halfway point, turn the bacon rashers with silicone-tipped tongs to promote even cooking.
5. Arrange everything on a plate and serve with canned white beans.
6. Bon appétit!

Egg Keto Muffins with Spinach

Prep time: 5 minutes / Cook time: 12 minutes / Serves 6

Ingredients

- 6 large eggs, lightly beaten
- 100g double cream
- 200g baby spinach
- 2 garlic cloves, minced
- 1/2 tsp red pepper flakes, crushed
- Sea salt and ground black pepper, to taste

Instructions

1. Start by preheating your Ninja Dual Zone Air Fryer to 180°C for 5 minutes. Now, lightly butter 6 muffin cases.

2. In a mixing bowl, thoroughly combine all the ingredients.
3. Spoon the mixture into the prepared muffin cases. Place 4 muffin cases in each drawer.
4. Select zone 1 and pair it with "BAKE" at 180°C for 12 minutes or until cooked through. Select "MATCH" followed by the "START/STOP" button.
5. Let the egg cups sit for about 5 minutes before unmolding and serving. Enjoy!

Roasted Potatoes with Eggs

Prep time: 5 minutes / Cook time: 22 minutes / Serves 4

Ingredients
- 600g yellow potatoes, diced
- 1 tbsp butter, room temperature
- 1 bell pepper, seeded and chopped
- 1 chilli pepper, seeded and chopped
- Sea salt and ground black pepper, to taste
- 1 tsp dried rosemary
- 1 tsp garlic granules
- 1 tsp onion powder
- 4 medium eggs

Instructions
1. Toss the potatoes with butter, peppers, and spices.
2. Whisk the eggs with salt and black pepper and pour the mixture into 4 silicone muffin cases (or two large ramekins).
3. Add potatoes to the zone 1 drawer; add the muffin cases (or ramekins) to the zone 2 drawer.
4. Select zone 1 and pair it with "ROAST" at 190°C for 22 minutes. Select zone 2 and pair it with "AIR FRY" at 180°C for 10 minutes
5. Select "SYNC" followed by the "START/STOP" button. At the halfway point, shake the drawer with potatoes to promote even cooking.
6. Bon appétit!

Breakfast Filo Parcels

Prep time: 10 minutes / Cook time: 10 minutes / Serves 8

Ingredients
- 8 (about 350g) rectangular sheets of filo pastry
- 400g smoked sausage, chopped
- 8 sundried tomatoes, chopped
- 2000g mozzarella, chopped
- 20g butter, melted

Instructions
1. Start by preheating your Ninja Dual Zone Air Fryer to 180°C for 5 minutes.
2. Pile up the filo pastry on a flat surface. Now, cut it into 4x4-inch squares.
3. In a mixing bowl, thoroughly combine the sausages, tomatoes, and mozzarella.
4. Divide the mixture between filo squares. Bring all 4 corners of the squares together; then, press the corners to seal them.
5. Brush the parcels with melted butter. Arrange the parcels in both drawers.
6. Select zone 1 and pair it with "BAKE" at 180°C for 10 minutes or until golden. Select "MATCH" followed by the "START/STOP" button.
7. Serve with a topping of choice and enjoy!

Baked Oatmeal

Prep time: 5 minutes / Cook time: 20 minutes / Serves 6

Ingredients
- 1 tsp peanut oil (or coconut oil)
- 300g old-fashioned oats
- 1 tbsp chia seeds
- 1 large egg, beaten
- 1/3 cup apple sauce
- 1 cup full-fat coconut milk
- 100g blackberries
- 1 tsp baking powder
- 50ml honey
- 1 tsp vanilla bean paste
- A pinch of sea salt
- A pinch of ground cinnamon
- 2 tbsp almond, chopped (optional)

Instructions
1. Brush the inside of two oven-safe baking tins with oil. Thoroughly combine all the Ingredients and spoon the mixture into the baking tins.
2. Select zone 1 and pair it with "BAKE" at 180°C for 20 minutes. Select "MATCH" to duplicate settings across both zones. Press the "START/STOP" button.
3. When zone 1 time reaches 10 minutes, turn the baking tin and reinsert the drawers to continue cooking.
4. Devour!

Spicy Hash Browns

Prep time: 10 minutes / Cook time: 30 minutes / Serves 6-8

Ingredients

- 600g potatoes (such as Maris Pipers or King Edward)
- Sea salt and ground black pepper, to taste
- 1 tsp chilli pepper flakes
- 50g butter, melted

Instructions

1. Boil the potatoes for 15 minutes; drain. Peel the potatoes and coarsely grate them into a bowl. Season them with salt, black pepper, and chilli pepper.
2. Add the melted butter to the mixture and mix to combine; divide the mixture between 6 to 8 lightly greased muffin cases.
3. Arrange the muffin cases in both drawers.
4. Select zone 1 and pair it with "AIR FRY" at 200°C for 15 minutes. Select "MATCH" followed by the "START/STOP" button.
5. Serve with your favourite tomato sauce. Enjoy!

Mini Frittatas

Prep time: 10 minutes / Cook time: 15 minutes / Serves 6

Ingredients

- 8 medium eggs
- 50g double cream
- 50g cream cheese
- 2 green onions, chopped
- 200g brown mushrooms, chopped
- 1/2 tsp cayenne pepper, or more to taste
- 1 tsp dried oregano
- Sea salt and ground black pepper, to taste

Instructions

1. Preheat your Ninja Dual Zone Air Fryer to 180°C for 5 minutes. Brush silicone cases with nonstick oil.
2. In a bowl, whisk the eggs until frothy; fold in the cream and cheese and mix to combine well. Add the other Ingredients and mix until everything is well incorporated.
3. Spoon the batter into the prepared silicone cases. Add them to the drawers.
4. Select zone 1 and pair it with "BAKE" at 180°C for 15 minutes. Select "MATCH" followed by the "START/STOP" button.
5. Bon appétit!

Breakfast Wraps

Prep time: 10 minutes / Cook time: 21 minutes / Serves 6

Ingredients

- 300g breakfast sausage, sliced
- 2 medium courgettes, sliced
- 1 tsp olive oil
- 1 tsp cayenne pepper
- 1/2 tsp garlic powder
- Sea salt and ground black pepper, to taste
- 6 medium tortilla wraps
- 1 bell pepper, seeded and sliced
- 100g canned beans, drained

Instructions

1. Insert a crisper plate in both drawers. Spray the plates with nonstick cooking oil.
2. Add breakfast sausage to the zone 1 drawer.
3. Toss the courgettes with olive oil, cayenne pepper, garlic powder, salt, and black pepper; then, add the courgettes to the zone 2 drawer.
4. Select zone 1 and pair it with "AIR FRY" at 200°C for 16 minutes. Select zone 2 and pair it with "AIR FRY" at 180°C for 10 minutes
5. Select "SYNC" followed by the "START/STOP" button. At the halfway point, shake the drawers to promote even cooking.
6. To assemble your wraps: divide the sausages, courgettes, pepper, and canned beans between tortilla wraps; wrap them up.
7. Add wraps to the drawers of your Ninja Dual Zone Air Fryer. Select "REHEAT" at 170°C for 5 minutes. Enjoy!

Sausage Rolls

Prep time: 10 minutes / Cook time: 10 minutes / Serves 6

Ingredients

- 375g puff pastry
- 2 tbsp plain flour, for dusting
- 2 tbsp tomato ketchup
- 1 tbsp English mustard
- 400g sausagemeat, crumbled
- 1 egg, beaten

Instructions

1. Dust a working surface with flour and roll out the pastry to a 35 x 30 cm rectangle. After precisely trimming the edges, cut the piece in half lengthwise to create two long strips. Leave a border around the sides and spread the ketchup and mustard in a thin layer.
2. Squeeze together the sausagemeat with 3 tbsp of cold water in a large dish.
3. Divide the mixture into two pieces and mould each

half into a cylindrical shape. Add each portion of meat to the middle of a pastry strip.

4. With the beaten egg, brush the pastry border. Use a fork to press the pastry edges together after folding one edge over the meat and rolling it up to enclose it.

5. Cut the sausage rolls into 5cm lengths and lower them onto two lined baking trays.

6. Select zone 1 and pair it with "BAKE" at 180°C for 10 minutes or until golden. Select "MATCH" followed by the "START/STOP" button.

7. Devour!

Chocolate Granola

Prep time: 10 minutes / Cook time: 15 minutes / Serves 10-12

Ingredients

* 200g rolled oats
* 100g cornflakes
* 100g almonds, roughly chopped (or hazelnuts)
* 40g coconut oil
* 50g clear honey
* 50g sunflower seeds
* 80g pumpkin seeds
* 1 tsp ground cinnamon
* A pinch of coarse sea salt
* 100g chocolate, chopped or shaved

Instructions

1. Preheat your Ninja Dual Zone Air Fryer to 180°C. Line two roasting tins with baking paper.

2. Mix the oats, cornflakes, almonds, coconut oil, and 20g of honey. Spread the mixture onto a roasting tin and add the roasting tin to the zone 1 drawer.

3. Mix the seeds with the remaining 20g of honey, cinnamon, and salt; spread the mixture onto the second roasting tin and add it to the zone 2 drawer.

4. Select zone 1 and pair it with "ROAST" at 170°C for 15 minutes. Select zone 2 and pair it with "ROAST" at 160°C for 9 minutes. Select "SYNC" followed by the "START/STOP" button.

5. When zone 1 time reaches 7 minutes, stir the ingredients, and reinsert the drawer to continue cooking.

6. When zone 2 time reaches 4 minutes, stir the ingredients, and reinsert the drawer to continue cooking.

7. Lastly, combine the oat mixture and the seed mixture; add chocolate to the warm granola and gently stir to combine. Devour!

Easy Filo Triangles

Prep time: 10 minutes / Cook time: 10 minutes / Serves 6-8

Ingredients

* 6 sheets filo pastry
* 60g melted butter
* 100g brie, chopped
* 6 tbsp strawberry jam

Instructions

1. Brush filo pastry with butter and cut each sheet lengthways into 2 strips.

2. Add brie and strawberry jam to the top of each strip; fold each over diagonally to make triangles.

3. Arrange the triangles in both drawers.

4. Select zone 1 and pair it with "BAKE" at 180°C for 10 minutes or until golden. Select "MATCH" followed by the "START/STOP" button.

5. Serve with a topping of choice and enjoy!

Hot Buns

Prep time: 10 minutes / Cook time: 19 minutes / Serves 6

Ingredients

* 200g cooked ham slices
* 500g button mushrooms, halved
* 1/2 tsp red pepper flakes, crushed
* Sea salt and ground black pepper, to taste
* 1 tsp oregano
* 1 tsp olive oil
* 1 large tomato, sliced
* 1 tbsp English mustard
* 6 medium sandwich buns

Instructions

1. Insert a crisping plate in both drawers. Add ham to the zone 1 drawer.

2. Toss the mushrooms with red pepper flakes, salt, black pepper, oregano, and olive oil until they are well coated on all sides. Put the mushrooms into the zone 2 drawer.

3. Select zone 1 and pair it with "AIR FRY" at 180°C for 10 minutes. Select zone 2 and pair it with "ROAST" at 190°C for 15 minutes. Select "SYNC" followed by the "START/STOP" button.

4. Divide the ham, mushrooms, tomato, and mustard among the sandwich buns.

5. Now, arrange the assembled sandwich buns in both drawers in your Ninja Dual Zone Air Fryer. Select "REHEAT" at 170°C for 4 minutes. Enjoy!

Hard-Boiled Eggs on Toast

Prep time: 5 minutes / Cook time: 15 minutes / Serves 5

Ingredients
- 5 large eggs
- Sea salt and ground black pepper, to taste
- 5 slices sourdough bread

Instructions
1. Preheat your Ninja Dual Zone Air Fryer to 130°C.
2. Add the eggs to the zone 1 drawer. Put the bread into the zone 2 drawer.
3. Select zone 1 and pair it with "BAKE" at 130°C for 15 minutes. Select zone 2 and pair it with "BAKE" at 190°C for 6 minutes. Select "SYNC" followed by the "START/STOP" button.
4. When zone 2 time reaches 3 minutes, turn the bread slices over, and reinsert the drawer to continue cooking. Cook until your toast is golden brown.
5. Remove the eggs and plunge them into an ice bath to stop cooking. Peel them and season with salt and pepper to taste.
6. Serve sliced eggs on toast and enjoy!

Egg Wraps with Chickpeas and Avocado

Prep time: 5 minutes / Cook time: 13 minutes / Serves 4

Ingredients
- 6 large eggs
- 6 tbsp porridge oats
- 2 tbsp whole milk
- Sea salt and red pepper flakes, to taste
- A small handful of chopped fresh parsley
- 2 handfuls of rocket lettuce
- 6 tbsp canned chickpeas, drained
- 1 large avocado, pitted and sliced

Instructions
1. Preheat your Ninja Dual Zone Air Fryer to 180°C. Very lightly butter two oval baking tins.
2. Beat the eggs with oats, milk, salt, pepper, and parsley. Spoon the mixture into the prepared baking tins. Place the tins in the drawers.
3. Select zone 1 and pair it with "BAKE" at 180°C for 13 minutes. Select "MATCH" followed by the "START/STOP" button.
4. Tip your egg wraps onto a plate, add rocket, chickpeas, and avocado; roll them up. Bon appétit!

Rocket and Pecorino Bruschetta

Prep time: 5 minutes / Cook time: 4 minutes / Serves 4

Ingredients
- 8 small slices of crusty bread
- 2 tbsp extra-virgin olive oil
- 1 large garlic clove, peeled
- 2 medium tomatoes, chopped
- 2 tbsp black olives, pitted and sliced
- 60g pecorino, sliced
- A pinch of chilli flakes
- Sea salt and ground black pepper, to taste
- A small handful of fresh mint leaves

Instructions
1. Brush the bread on both sides with olive oil.
2. Place bread slices in zone 1 and zone 2 drawers. Select zone 1 and pair it with "BAKE" at 180°C for 2 minutes. Select "MATCH" to duplicate settings across both zones. Press the "START/STOP" button.
3. Rub garlic on toasted bread slices and top them with the remaining ingredients, except for the mint leaves.
4. Select zone 1 and pair it with "BAKE" at 180°C for 2 minutes. Select "MATCH" to duplicate settings across both zones. Press the "START/STOP" button.
5. Garnish your bruschetta with fresh mint leaves.
6. Bon appétit!

Chicory Polenta Tart with Sausage

Prep time: 5 minutes / Cook time: 20 minutes / Serves 6

Ingredients
- 600ml vegetable broth
- 200g quick-cook polenta
- 1 tbsp olive
- 4 smoked sausages, sliced
- 180g cheddar cheese, thinly sliced
- 2 heads of red chicory, halved
- 1/2 tsp chilli flakes
- Sea salt and ground black pepper, to taste

Instructions
1. Bring the broth to a rapid boil in a deep saucepan; immediately turn the heat to a medium-low. Gradually and carefully, stir in the polenta and olive oil.
2. Let it simmer, for about 5 minutes, uncovered, whisking continuously to avoid lumps. Pour your polenta into two lightly greased baking trays and let it cool completely.
3. Add baking trays to the drawers.

4. Select zone 1 and pair it with "BAKE" at 190°C for 20 minutes. Select "MATCH" to duplicate settings across both zones. Press the "START/STOP" button.
5. At the halfway point, add sausages and cheese; reinsert the drawers to continue cooking.
6. Top polenta tarts with the remaining Ingredients and serve warm or at room temperature. Bon appétit!

Breakfast Sausage with Soft-Boiled Eggs

Prep time: 5 minutes / Cook time: 15 minutes / Serves 4

Ingredients
- 4 pork sausages
- 4 large eggs
- 1/4 teaspoon sweet smoked paprika, or more to taste
- Sea salt and ground black pepper, to taste
- A small bunch of parsley, chopped

Instructions
1. Pierce the sausages all over using a sharp knife to help release more fat. Add the sausages to the zone 1 drawer. Put the eggs into the zone 2 drawer.
2. Select zone 1 and pair it with "AIR FRY" at 200°C for 15 minutes. Select zone 2 and pair it with "AIR FRY" at 130°C for 10 to 12 minutes. Select "SYNC" followed by the "START/STOP" button.
3. When zone 2 time reaches 8 minutes, shake the basket, and reinsert the drawer to continue cooking.
4. Remove the eggs and plunge them into an ice bath to stop cooking. Peel them and season with paprika, salt, and black pepper to taste.
5. Serve warm sausages with eggs on the side, garnish with fresh parsley, and enjoy!

Easy Breakfast Wraps

Prep time:10 minutes / Cook time: 21 minutes / Serves 5

Ingredients
- 400g breakfast sausage, sliced
- 500g button mushrooms, cut in quarters
- 1 tsp olive oil
- Sea salt and ground black pepper, to taste
- 1/2 tsp garlic powder
- 5 tortilla wraps
- 1 bell pepper, seeded and sliced
- 100g canned chickpeas, drained

Instructions
1. Insert a crisper plate in both drawers. Spray the plates with nonstick cooking oil.
2. Add breakfast sausage to the zone 1 drawer.
3. Toss the mushrooms with olive oil, salt, black pepper, and garlic powder; now, add the mushrooms to the zone 2 drawer.
4. Select zone 1 and pair it with "AIR FRY" at 200°C for 16 minutes. Select zone 2 and pair it with "AIR FRY" at 200°C for 12 minutes
5. Select "SYNC" followed by the "START/STOP" button. At the halfway point, shake your food or toss it with silicone-tipped tongs to promote even cooking.
6. To assemble your wraps: divide the sausages, mushrooms, pepper, and chickpeas between tortilla wraps; wrap them up.
7. Add wraps to the drawers of your Ninja Foodi. Select "REHEAT" at 170°C for 5 minutes. Devour!

Breakfast Hash Browns

Prep time:20 minutes / Cook time: 15minutes / Serves 4

Ingredients
- 500g medium-sized potatoes (such as Maris Pipers or King Edward)
- Sea salt and ground black pepper, to taste
- 1 tsp cayenne pepper
- 50g butter, melted

Instructions
1. Boil the potatoes for 10 minutes; drain until they are cool enough to handle. Peel the potatoes and coarsely grate them into a bowl. Season your potatoes with salt and pepper.
2. Add the melted butter and mix to combine; shape the mixture into 7-8 patties. Insert a crisper plate in both drawers.
3. Spray the plates with nonstick cooking oil. Arrange hash browns on crisper plates
4. Select zone 1 and pair it with "AIR FRY" at 200°C for 15 minutes. Select "MATCH" followed by the "START/STOP" button.
5. At the halfway point, turn the hash browns over with silicone-tipped tongs. Reinsert drawers to resume cooking.
6. Serve warm and enjoy!

CHAPTER 2 BEANS & GRAINS

Country-Style Shortbread

Prep time: 10 minutes / Cook time: 30 minutes / Serves 8

Ingredients

- 250g all-purpose flour
- 230g butter, room temperature
- 120g confectioners' sugar
- 1/4 tsp ground cinnamon
- 1 tsp pure vanilla extract
- A pinch of coarse sea salt

Instructions

1. Start by preheating your Ninja Dual Zone Air Fryer to 160°C for 5 minutes.
2. Line two baking tins with baking parchment. Using your fingertips, rub the flour and butter together until it resembles fine breadcrumbs.
3. After that, stir in the sugar, cinnamon, vanilla, and salt.
4. Tip the mixture into the prepared tins in an even layer; now, press the mixture down firmly with the back of a spoon.
5. Then, using a fork, prick the dough in a random pattern to prevent the shortbread from bubbling as it bakes. Add the prepared tins to the drawers.
6. Select zone 1 and pair it with "BAKE" at 160°C for 30 minutes. Select "MATCH" followed by the "START/STOP" button.
7. Bake until it is golden brown around the edges. Leave to cool completely in the tin before serving and enjoy!

Roasted Garbanzo Beans

Prep time: 10 minutes / Cook time: 15 minutes / Serves 6

Ingredients

- 400g garbanzo beans, canned or boiled, drained
- 1 tbsp olive oil
- 1 tsp red pepper flakes
- Sea salt and ground black pepper, to taste

Instructions

1. Start by preheating your Ninja Dual Zone Air Fryer to 190°C for 5 minutes.
2. Arrange the garbanzo beans in parchment-lined drawers.
3. Select zone 1 and pair it with "ROAST" at 190°C for 15 minutes. Select "MATCH" to duplicate settings across both zones. Press the "START/STOP" button.
4. When zone 1 time reaches 8 minutes, shake the basket to ensure even browning; reinsert the drawers to continue cooking.
5. Enjoy!

Cannellini Bean Salad

Prep time: 10 minutes / Cook time: 15 minutes / Serves 4-5

Ingredients

- 400g canned cannellini beans, drained and rinsed
- 2 tbsp extra-virgin olive oil
- Sea salt and ground black pepper, to taste
- 100g cherry tomatoes
- 2 bell peppers, seeded and halved
- 1 shallot, sliced
- 1 fresh garlic clove, minced
- 2 tbsp fresh parsley leaves, chopped
- 2 tbsp fresh lime (or lemon) juice

Instructions

1. Toss the cannellini beans with 1 tablespoon of olive oil, salt, and black pepper.
2. Place the cannellini beans in the zone 1 drawer. Place cherry tomatoes and peppers in the zone 2 drawer and spray them with nonstick cooking oil.
3. Select zone 1 and pair it with "ROAST" at 190°C for 15 minutes. Select "MATCH" to duplicate settings across both zones. Press the "START/STOP" button.
4. When zone 1 time reaches 7 minutes, shake the basket to ensure even browning; reinsert the drawers to continue cooking.
5. Cut the roasted peppers into slices. Toss roasted beans, cherry tomatoes, and peppers in a salad bowl; add the other Ingredients and toss to combine well.
6. Bon appétit!

Granola with a Twist

Prep time: 10 minutes / Cook time: 15 minutes / Serves 10-12

Ingredients

- 300g rolled oats
- 50g shredded coconut
- 100g walnuts, chopped

- 40g tahini paste
- 1 tsp ground cloves
- 1 tsp ground cinnamon
- 1 tsp ground cardamom
- 50ml date syrup
- 50g sunflower seeds
- 100g dried figs, chopped

Instructions

1. Preheat your Ninja Dual Zone Air Fryer to 180°C. Line two roasting tins with baking paper.
2. Mix all the ingredients, except dried figs, in a bowl. Spread the mixture onto roasting tins and add them to the drawers.
3. Select zone 1 and pair it with "ROAST" at 170°C for 15 minutes. Select "MATCH" to duplicate settings across both zones. Press the "START/STOP" button.
4. At the halfway point, stir the Ingredients with a wooden spoon, and reinsert the drawers to continue cooking.
5. Lastly, combine the mixture with dried figs. Enjoy!

Fluffy Oat Pancakes

Prep time: 10 minutes / Cook time: 20 minutes / Serves 4

Ingredients

- 1 tsp butter, melted
- 2 medium bananas, mashed
- 1250ml whole milk
- 2 large eggs, separated
- 200g rolled oats
- 1 tsp bicarbonate of soda
- 1 tsp baking powder
- 1 tsp fresh ginger, peeled and grated
- 1 tsp vanilla bean paste
- A pinch of salt
- A few drizzles of fresh lemon juice

Instructions

1. Brush two baking tins with melted butter. Thoroughly combine all the Ingredients and spoon the mixture into the baking tins.
2. Add the baking tins to the drawers.
3. Select zone 1 and pair it with "BAKE" at 190°C for 20 minutes. Select "MATCH" to duplicate settings across both zones. Press the "START/STOP" button.
4. Serve with toppings of choice and enjoy!

Flapjacks with Seeds

Prep time: 10 minutes / Cook time: 20 minutes / Serves 8-10

Ingredients

- 300g old-fashioned rolled oats
- 100g agave syrup
- 1 tbsp flax seeds
- 1 tbsp sesame seeds
- 2 tbsp hemp seeds, hulled
- 100g peanut butter
- A pinch of sea salt
- A pinch of grated nutmeg
- 1/2 tsp cinnamon powder

Instructions

1. Start by preheating your Ninja Dual Zone Air Fryer to 175°C. Now, brush muffin cases with nonstick cooking spray.
2. In your processor, mix the rolled oats with the other ingredients.
3. Divide the batter between the prepared muffin cases. Lower the muffin cases into the drawers.
4. Select zone 1 and pair it with "BAKE" at 180°C for 20 minutes. Select "MATCH" followed by the "START/STOP" button.
5. Allow your flapjacks to cool for about 10 minutes before unmolding. Enjoy!

Acai Berry Brownies

Prep time: 10 minutes / Cook time: 35 minutes / Serves 8-10

- Ingredients
- 100g plain flour
- 50g rolled oats
- 300g golden caster sugar
- 1/2 tsp cinnamon powder
- 100g butter, room temperature
- 100g peanut butter
- 4 medium eggs
- 200g dark chocolate chunks
- 150g acai berries

Instructions

1. Line two baking tins with baking paper.
2. In a mixing bowl, thoroughly combine the flour, oats, sugar, and cinnamon powder.
3. Then, gradually and slowly, stir the wet mixture into the dry mixture, and mix until creamy and uniform. Fold in the chocolate chunks and berries.
4. Spoon the batter into the prepared baking tins.
5. Select zone 1 and pair it with "BAKE" at 160°C for 35 minutes. Select "MATCH" followed by the "START/STOP" button.

6. Check your brownies for doneness using a toothpick. Cool before slicing into squares and enjoy!

Mexican-Style Pasta Bake

Prep time: 5 minutes / Cook time: 21 minutes / Serves 6

Ingredients

- 400g pasta of choice
- 1 tbsp olive oil
- 600g skinless chicken breasts, chopped
- 1 large onion, chopped
- 1 large carrot, trimmed and chopped
- 2 small garlic cloves, crushed
- 2 (400g) cans tomatoes, chopped
- 1 sweet bell pepper, seeded and chopped
- 1 chilli pepper, seeded and chopped
- 100ml vegetable stock
- 100ml tomato purée
- 100ml double cream
- 100g canned black beans, drained and rinsed
- 1/4 tsp chilli powder
- 1/2 tsp Mexican oregano
- 1 tsp ground coriander
- 1 heaped tsp sweet smoked paprika

Instructions

1. Remove a crisper plate from your Ninja Dual Zone Air Fryer. Brush two baking tins with nonstick oil.
2. Cook pasta according to the manufacturer's Instructions.
3. Meanwhile, heat olive oil in a nonstick frying pan over a medium-high flame. Cook chicken chunks for about 3 minutes, until no longer pink.
4. In the same pan, sauté the onion and carrot for about 3 minutes, until tender and translucent; add garlic and continue sauteing for 30 seconds more, until aromatic.
5. Add the sauteed chicken mixture to the pasta; stir in the remaining ingredients. Spoon the mixture into prepared baking tins and add the tins to your Ninja Dual Zone Air Fryer.
6. Select zone 1 and pair it with "BAKE" at 180°C for 15 minutes. Select "MATCH" followed by the "START/STOP" button.
7. When zone 1 time reaches 10 minutes, gently stir to promote even cooking; reinsert the drawers to continue cooking. Enjoy!

French Toast with Jam

Prep time: 10 minutes / Cook time: 13-15 minutes / Serves 6

Ingredients

- Cooking oil
- 6 tbsp whole milk
- 3 medium eggs
- 2 tbsp golden caster sugar
- 2 tbsp butter, room temperature
- 6 thick white bread
- 6 tbsp jam of choice

Instructions

1. Start by preheating your Ninja Dual Zone Air Fryer to 180°C for 5 minutes.
2. Spray drawers with cooking oil; now, line the base with a sheet of baking paper.
3. In a mixing bowl, whisk the milk, eggs, sugar, and butter. Dip bread slices in the custard mixture until they are well coated on all sides. Arrange French toast in the drawers.
4. Select zone 1 and pair it with "AIR FRYER" at 180°C for 13 to 15 minutes. Select "MATCH" followed by the "START/STOP" button.
5. When zone 1 time reaches 7 minutes, turn the bread slices over; reinsert the drawers to continue cooking.
6. Serve French toast with your favourite jam. Bon appétit!

Ricotta Raisin Bagels

Prep time: 10 minutes / Cook time: 6 minutes / Serves 6

Ingredients

- 160g ricotta
- 4 tsp honey
- 1/2 tsp cinnamon, ground
- 4 raisin bagels
- 4 dried figs, chopped

Instructions

1. Add your bagels to both drawers of your Ninja Dual Zone Air Fryer.
2. Select zone 1 and pair it with "BAKE" at 180°C for 6 minutes. Select "MATCH" followed by the "START/STOP" button.
3. When zone 1 time reaches 3 minutes, turn the bagels over, and then, reinsert the drawers to continue cooking. Cook until your bagels are golden brown and fragrant.
4. Thoroughly combine the ricotta with the honey and cinnamon; now, spread the mixture over the cut sides of the toasted raisin bagel. Top them with sliced figs before closing the sandwich.
5. Repeat with the other bagels, serve immediately, and

enjoy!

Classic Chilli Con Carne

Prep time: 10 minutes / Cook time: 20 minutes / Serves 6

Ingredients
- 2 tsp olive oil
- 500g lean minced beef
- 1 large carrot, chopped
- 1 medium onion, chopped
- 2 bell peppers, seeded and chopped
- 1 tsp hot chilli powder
- 1 tbsp dried Mexican oregano
- 1 tsp paprika
- 1 tsp ground cumin
- 1 bay leaf
- 1 beef stock cube
- 1 (400g) can tomatoes, crushed
- 2 (400g) cans of kidney beans, drained and rinsed

Instructions
1. Heat 1 teaspoon of olive oil in a sauté pan over medium-high heat. Once hot, cook the beef until no longer pink, or about 3 minutes.
2. Then, sauté the carrot, onion, and peppers for about 3 minutes, until just tender.
3. Brush the inside of two oven-safe baking tins with the remaining olive oil. Add the remaining ingredients, along with 500ml of water, to the meat mixture and gently stir to combine.
4. Spoon the mixture into the prepared baking tins and add them to the drawers.
5. Select zone 1 and pair it with "AIR FRY" at 180°C for 20 minutes. Select "MATCH" to duplicate settings across both zones. Press the "START/STOP" button.
6. When zone 1 time reaches 10 minutes, stir the beans, and reinsert the drawers to continue cooking.
7. Bon appétit!

Garbanzo Bean Salad

Prep time: 10 minutes / Cook time: 13 minutes / Serves 4-5

Ingredients
- 400g canned garbanzo beans, drained and rinsed
- 2 tbsp extra-virgin olive oil
- 1/2 tsp cayenne pepper
- Sea salt and ground black pepper, to taste
- 1 medium courgette, sliced
- 1 head rocket lettuce, shredded
- 1 small onion, sliced
- 2 tbsp fresh lemon juice
- 1 tsp clear honey
- 1 garlic clove, finely grated
- 2 tbsp fresh parsley leaves, chopped
- 1/4 tsp ground cumin

Instructions
1. Toss the garbanzo beans with 1 tablespoon of olive oil, cayenne pepper, salt, and black pepper.
2. Place the garbanzo beans in the zone 1 drawer. Place courgette slices in the zone 2 drawer and spray them with nonstick cooking oil.
3. Select zone 1 and pair it with "ROAST" at 180°C for 13 minutes. Select "MATCH" to duplicate settings across both zones. Press the "START/STOP" button.
4. When zone 1 time reaches 6 minutes, shake the basket to ensure even browning; reinsert the drawers to continue cooking.
5. Toss roasted garbanzo beans with other vegetables in a salad bowl; mix the remaining 1 tablespoon of olive oil, lemon juice, honey, garlic, parsley, and cumin.
6. Dress your salad, toss to combine and enjoy!

Healthy Porridge Bowl

Prep time: 10 minutes / Cook time: 22 minutes / Serves 5

Ingredients
- 2 tsp butter, melted
- 360g millet grains, soaked overnight, drained, and rinsed
- 700ml milk
- 1 cinnamon stick
- 2 tbsp smooth almond butter
- 100g dried figs, pitted and chopped
- 2 large bananas, peeled and mashed
- 1/2 tsp vanilla bean

Instructions
1. Grease the inside of four ramekins with butter.
2. Tip the millet into a deep saucepan; pour in the milk and 600ml of water. Add the cinnamon stick to the saucepan.
3. Bring it to a boil. Reduce the heat to medium-low and leave to simmer until the millet is tender (it will take about 10 minutes).
4. Now, combine the millet porridge with the other Ingredients and spoon the mixture into the ramekins. Add the ramekins to the drawers.
5. Select zone 1 and pair it with "BAKE" at 180°C for 12 minutes. Select "MATCH" to duplicate settings across both zones. Press the "START/STOP" button.

6. Bon appétit!

Cheddar Cornbread

Prep time: 10 minutes / Cook time: 25 minutes / Serves 10

Ingredients
- 3 small eggs
- 50ml olive oil
- 100g sweetcorn kernels
- 100ml milk
- 200ml pot buttermilk
- 150g plain flour
- 150g polenta or cornmeal
- 1 tsp baking powder
- 50g cheddar cheese, grated

Instructions
1. Lightly spray two baking tins with cooking oil.
2. In a mixing bowl, thoroughly combine the dry ingredients; in a separate bowl, mix the liquid ingredients.
3. Add the liquid mixture to the dry Ingredients and whisk until everything is well incorporated. Fold in the grated cheddar.
4. Spoon the mixture into the prepared baking tins, and lower them into the drawers.
5. Select zone 1 and pair it with "BAKE" at 180°C for 25 minutes, until golden brown. Select "MATCH" to duplicate settings across both zones. Press the "START/STOP" button.
6. Test your cornbread for doneness using a toothpick. Cool in the tins for 10 minutes, then, turn out and cut into squares. Bon appétit!

Refried Bean Chorizo Quesadillas

Prep time: 10 minutes / Cook time: 8 minutes / Serves 4

Ingredients
- 300g refried beans, drained and warmed
- 160g chorizo, sliced
- 4 tbsp mayonnaise
- 50ml fresh salsa
- 4 large flour tortillas
- 2 tsp olive oil

Instructions
1. Begin by preheating your Ninja Dual Zone Air Fryer to 180°C for 5 minutes.
2. Divide refried beans, chorizo, mayonnaise, and salsa between two tortillas. Top with the remaining 2 tortillas and fold in half.

3. Add them to the lightly-greased drawers. Brush your quesadillas with 1 teaspoon of olive oil.
4. Select zone 1 and pair it with "BAKE" at 180°C for 8 minutes. Select "MATCH" followed by the "START/STOP" button.
5. When zone 1 time reaches 4 minutes, turn your quesadillas over and brush them with the remaining 1 teaspoon of olive oil on the other side; reinsert the drawers to continue cooking.
6. Cut your quesadillas into halves and serve warm.
7. Devour!

Sausage Rolls

Prep time: 10 minutes / Cook time: 10 minutes / Serves 4

Ingredients
- 1 package croissant dough
- 200g breakfast sausages, casing removed
- 2 tbsp red onion chutney
- 1 tbsp English mustard
- 1 egg, beaten
- 2 tbsp whole milk

Instructions
1. Roll out the croissant dough and use a knife to separate the triangles. Mix the sausage meat with red onion chutney and English mustard until well combined.
2. Place the sausage mixture on half of the rolls, making sure to leave 1/2-inch from the edges.
3. Now, roll the dough to form crescents; pinch to seal the edges. Beat the egg with milk and glaze the rolls with the egg wash.
4. Select zone 1 and pair it with "BAKE" at 180°C for 10 minutes. Select "MATCH" followed by the "START/STOP" button.
5. When zone 1 time reaches 5 minutes, turn the sausage rolls over and brush them with the remaining egg wash on the other side; reinsert the drawers to continue cooking.
6. Bon appétit!

Homemade Club Sandwiches

Prep time: 10 minutes / Cook time: 25 minutes / Serves 3

Ingredients
- 4 medium eggs
- 4 slices ham, cooked
- 1 tsp Dijon mustard

- 4 tbsp mayonnaise, regular
- 1 tomato, sliced
- Sea salt and ground black pepper, to taste
- 6 thick-cut slices of sourdough bread

Instructions

1. Preheat your Ninja Dual Zone Air Fryer to 130°C.
2. Add the eggs to the zone 1 drawer. Put the ham into the zone 2 drawer.
3. Select zone 1 and pair it with "BAKE" at 130°C for 15 minutes. Select zone 2 and pair it with "AIR FRY" at 180°C for 6 minutes. Select "SYNC" followed by the "START/STOP" button.
4. When zone 2 time reaches 3 minutes, turn the ham over, and reinsert the drawer to continue cooking.
5. Remove the eggs and plunge them into an ice bath to stop cooking. Peel them and season with salt and black pepper to taste.
6. Assemble three sandwiches: place the mustard, mayo, tomatoes, eggs, and ham on 3 bread slices; top with the remaining slices of bread. Cut into halves and secure with cocktail sticks.
7. Arrange your sandwiches in the cooking basket. Select zone 1 and pair it with "BAKE" at 180°C for 10 minutes. Select "MATCH" followed by the "START/STOP" button.
8. Serve with crisps and enjoy!

Pecan Granola Bars

Prep time: 10 minutes / Cook time: 20 minutes / Serves 10

Ingredients

- 200g oats
- 20g coconut oil
- 20g sesame seeds
- 20g sunflower seeds
- 30g raw pepitas
- 100g pecans, roughly chopped
- 100g clear honey
- 100g prunes, pitted and chopped
- 1/2 tsp ground cinnamon
- 1/4 tsp ground cloves
- 1/2 tsp vanilla bean paste

Instructions

1. In a mixing bowl, thoroughly combine all the Ingredients, except the prunes.
2. Scrape the batter into two parchment-lined baking trays, pressing down lightly with a silicone spatula.
3. Select zone 1 and pair it with "BAKE" at 160°C

for 20 minutes. Select "MATCH" followed by the "START/STOP" button.
4. Let your granola cool on a wire rack before cutting it into bars.
5. Bon appétit!

Roasted Vegetable and Quinoa Bowl

Prep time: 10 minutes / Cook time: 22 minutes / Serves 4

Ingredients

- 330g quinoa, soaked overnight, drained, and rinsed
- 1 medium courgette, diced
- 2 bell peppers, seeded and halved
- 100g cherry tomatoes
- 1 small shallot, sliced
- 1 tbsp olive oil, room temperature
- 200 ml vegetable stock
- 1 bay leaf
- 1 dried rosemary sprig, leaves picked and chopped
- Ground black pepper, to taste

Instructions

1. Cook your quinoa according to the package Instructions. Toss vegetables with olive oil.
2. Arrange courgette and peppers in the zone 1 drawer. Then, place cherry tomatoes and shallot slices in the zone 2 drawer.
3. Select zone 1 and pair it with "ROAST" at 180°C for 12 minutes. Select zone 2 and pair it with "AIR FRY" at 180°C for 10 minutes. Select "SYNC" followed by the "START/STOP" button.
4. At the halfway point, shake the drawers to ensure even cooking. Then, reinsert the drawer to continue cooking.
5. Next, combine quinoa with roasted vegetables, vegetable stock, bay leaf, rosemary, and ground black pepper.
6. Divide the mixture between two lightly greased baking dishes. Select zone 1 and pair it with "BAKE" at 170°C for 10 minutes. Select "MATCH" to duplicate settings across both zones. Press the "START/STOP" button.
7. Bon appétit!

Garbanzo Beans with Sausage and Pancetta

Prep time: 10 minutes / Cook time: 20 minutes / Serves 6

Ingredients

- 2 tsp olive oil
- 1 large carrot, chopped

- 1 medium onion, chopped
- 2 bell peppers, seeded and chopped
- 1 tsp hot chilli powder
- 1 tsp cayenne pepper
- 1 bouquet garni
- 300ml vegetable broth
- 1 (400g) can tomatoes, crushed
- 2 (400g) cans garbanzo beans, drained and rinsed
- 200g smoked sausages, sliced
- 100g pancetta, cut into thin lardons

Instructions

1. Heat 1 teaspoon of olive oil in a sauté pan over medium-high heat. Once hot, sauté the carrot, onion, and peppers for about 3 minutes, until just tender.
2. Brush the inside of two oven-safe baking tins with the remaining 1 teaspoon of olive oil. Add the remaining Ingredients to the sauteed mixture and gently stir to combine.
3. Spoon the mixture into the prepared baking tins and add them to the drawers.
4. Select zone 1 and pair it with "BAKE" at 180°C for 20 minutes. Select "MATCH" to duplicate settings across both zones. Press the "START/STOP" button.
5. When zone 1 time reaches 10 minutes, stir the beans, and reinsert the drawers to continue cooking.
6. Bon appétit!

Classic Bean Curry

Prep time: 10 minutes / Cook time: 20 minutes / Serves 6

Ingredients

- 1 tbsp olive oil
- 1 medium leek, chopped
- 2 garlic cloves, finely chopped
- A thumb-sized piece of ginger, peeled and finely chopped
- 1 tsp turmeric powder
- 1 tsp ground cumin
- 1 tsp garam masala
- 1 bay leaf
- 400g canned beans, drained
- 400g can tomatoes, chopped

Instructions

1. Heat 1 teaspoon of olive oil in a sauté pan over medium-high heat. Sauté the leeks for about 3 minutes, until just tender.
2. Then, sauté the garlic and ginger for about 30 seconds, until fragrant.
3. Brush the inside of two oven-safe baking tins with cooking oil. Add the remaining Ingredients, along

with 300ml of water, to the bean mixture and gently stir to combine.
4. Spoon the mixture into the prepared baking tins and add them to the drawers.
5. Select zone 1 and pair it with "AIR FRY" at 180°C for 20 minutes. Select "MATCH" to duplicate settings across both zones. Press the "START/STOP" button.
6. When zone 1 time reaches 10 minutes, stir the beans, and reinsert the drawers to continue cooking.
7. Bon appétit!

Green Bean Mac 'n' Cheese

Prep time: 10 minutes / Cook time: 15 minutes / Serves 6

Ingredients

- 1 tbsp olive oil
- 4 tbsp wholemeal flour
- 500ml whole milk
- Sea salt and ground black pepper, to taste
- 1 tsp cayenne pepper
- 360g pasta tubes
- 350g fine green beans
- 150g mature cheddar, grated

Instructions

1. Heat the oil in a medium saucepan over medium heat. Now, add the flour and stir well. Gradually pour in a little of the milk, stirring continuously.
2. Cook and stir until you have a smooth, uniform sauce. Stir in the salt, black pepper, and cayenne pepper; reserve.
3. Bring a large pan of water to a rolling boil. Cook pasta tubes for 8 minutes. Now, add the green beans, and boil for 3 minutes more, until crisp-tender. Drain your pasta and the green beans.
4. Tip the mixture into two lightly greased gratin dishes. Pour over the reserved sauce.
5. Select zone 1 and pair it with "BAKE" at 200°C for 15 minutes. Select "MATCH" to duplicate settings across both zones. Press the "START/STOP" button.
6. When zone 1 time reaches 8 minutes, add cheese to the top. Reinsert the drawers to continue cooking. Cook until the top is bubbling and golden.
7. Bon appétit!

Turkey Pasta Bake

Prep time: 5 minutes / Cook time: 21 minutes / Serves 6

Ingredients

- 400g pasta of choice

- 1 tbsp olive oil
- 600g turkey mince
- 1 large onion, chopped
- 1 large bell pepper, trimmed and chopped
- 2 small garlic cloves, crushed
- 2 (400g) cans tomatoes, chopped
- 200ml chicken stock
- 100ml tomato purée
- 100g white beans, drained and rinsed
- 1/2 tsp oregano
- 1 tsp ground coriander

Instructions

1. Remove a crisper plate from your Ninja Dual Zone Air Fryer. Brush two baking tins with nonstick oil.
2. Cook pasta according to the manufacturer's Instructions.
3. Meanwhile, heat olive oil in a nonstick frying pan over a medium-high flame. Cook turkey mince for about 3 minutes, until no longer pink.
4. In the same pan, sauté the onion and pepper for about 3 minutes, until tender and translucent; add garlic and continue sauteing for 30 seconds more, until aromatic.
5. Add the turkey mixture to the pasta; stir in the remaining Ingredients. Spoon the mixture into prepared baking tins and add the tins to your Ninja Dual Zone Air Fryer.
6. Select zone 1 and pair it with "BAKE" at 180°C for 15 minutes. Select "MATCH" followed by the "START/STOP" button.
7. When zone 1 time reaches 10 minutes, gently stir to promote even cooking; reinsert the drawers to continue cooking. Cook until golden brown and bubbling.
8. Bon appétit!

Buckwheat Porridge

Prep time: 10 minutes / Cook time: 30 minutes / Serves 5

Ingredients

- 2 tsp coconut oil, room temperature
- 360g buckwheat, soaked overnight, drained, and rinsed
- 700ml milk
- 1 cinnamon stick
- 3-4 cloves
- 2 tbsp smooth almond butter
- 100g prunes, pitted and chopped
- 2 large bananas, peeled and mashed
- 1/2 tsp pure vanilla extract

Instructions

1. Grease the inside of four ramekins with coconut oil.

2. Tip the buckwheat into a deep saucepan; pour in the milk and 600ml of water. Add the cinnamon stick and cloves to the saucepan.
3. Bring it to a boil. Reduce the heat to medium-low and leave to simmer until the buckwheat is tender (it will take about 15 minutes).
4. Now, combine the buckwheat with the remaining Ingredients and divide the mixture between the prepared ramekins. Lower the ramekins into the drawers.
5. Select zone 1 and pair it with "BAKE" at 170°C for 15 minutes. Select "MATCH" to duplicate settings across both zones. Press the "START/STOP" button.
6. Bon appétit!

Sausage and Red Kidney Bean Chilli

Prep time: 10 minutes / Cook time: 20 minutes / Serves 6

Ingredients

- 2 tsp olive oil
- 200g Toulouse sausages, sliced
- 1 medium onion, chopped
- 2 bell peppers, seeded and chopped
- 1 tsp hot chilli powder
- 1 tsp cayenne pepper
- 1 bouquet garni
- 2 sage sprigs, leaves picked and chopped
- 300ml vegetable broth
- 1 (400g) can tomatoes, crushed
- 2 (400g) cans of red kidney beans, drained and rinsed
- 100g pancetta, cut into thin lardons

Instructions

1. Heat 1 teaspoon of olive oil in a sauté pan over medium-high heat. Cook sausages until slightly browned and cooked through about 4 minutes.
2. Then, sauté the onion and peppers for about 3 minutes, until just tender.
3. Brush the inside of two oven-safe dishes with the remaining 1 teaspoon of olive oil. Add the remaining Ingredients to the sausage mixture and gently stir to combine.
4. Spoon the mixture into the prepared dishes and add them to the drawers.
5. Select zone 1 and pair it with "BAKE" at 180°C for 20 minutes. Select "MATCH" to duplicate settings across both zones. Press the "START/STOP" button.
6. When zone 1 time reaches 10 minutes, stir your chilli, and reinsert the drawers to continue cooking. Serve warm and enjoy!

CHAPTER 3 FAMILY FAVOURITES (BRITISH CLASSICS)

Polenta Roasties

Prep time: 10 minutes / Cook time: 25 minutes / Serves 6

Ingredients
- 1.5kg potatoes, peeled and cut into bite-sized chunks
- 20ml olive oil
- 4 tbsp dried polenta

Instructions
1. Boil the potatoes in a saucepan for about 8 minutes.
2. Drain the potato chunks and toss them in the polenta. Tip the potatoes into the cooking basket.
3. Now, drizzle over the olive oil.
4. Select zone 1 and pair it with "ROAST" at 190°C for 25 minutes. Select "MATCH" to duplicate settings across both zones. Press the "START/STOP" button.
5. When zone 1 time reaches 12 minutes, shake the basket, and reinsert the drawers to continue cooking.
6. Serve warm and enjoy!

Fish Soufflé Tart

Prep time: 10 minutes / Cook time: 20 minutes / Serves 6

Ingredients
- 1 tsp olive oil
- 8 large eggs
- 2 tbsp double cream
- 200g smoked salmon
- 2 spring onions, chopped
- 2 garlic cloves, minced
- Sea salt and ground black pepper, to taste
- 2 tbsp fresh parsley, chopped
- 100g cheddar cheese, room temperature

Instructions
1. Brush the sides and bottom of two soufflé dishes with olive oil. Beat the eggs until pale and frothy; then, add in the double cream and mix to combine.
2. Add the salmon, onions, garlic, salt, pepper, and parsley; gently stir to combine.
3. Spoon the mixture into the prepared soufflé dishes, and smooth the top with a spatula.
4. Select zone 1 and pair it with "BAKE" at 180°C for 20 minutes. Select "MATCH" to duplicate settings across both zones. Press the "START/STOP" button.
5. When zone 1 time reaches 10 minutes, add cheddar to the top, and reinsert the drawers to continue cooking.
6. Bon appétit!

Roast Chicken with Vegetables

Prep time: 5 minutes / Cook time: 34 minutes / Serves 4

Ingredients
- 600g chicken breasts, skin-on, boneless
- Sea salt and ground black pepper
- 2 tbsp butter, room temperature
- 1 tsp garlic granules
- 1 tsp hot paprika
- 1 large onion, roughly chopped
- 2 large carrots, roughly chopped

Instructions
1. Toss the chicken with salt, pepper, 1 tablespoon of butter, garlic granules, and hot paprika.
2. Place the chicken in the zone 1 drawer. Then, toss the onion and carrots with salt, pepper, and the remaining 1 tablespoon of butter, and arrange them in the zone 2 drawer.
3. Select zone 1 and pair it with "ROAST" at 190°C for 34 minutes. Select zone 2 and pair it with "AIR FRY" at 200°C for about 16 minutes. Select "SYNC" followed by the "START/STOP" button.
4. At the halfway point, flip the Ingredients with silicone-tipped tongs to promote even browning. Reinsert drawers to resume cooking.
5. Serve warm and enjoy!

Traditional Cornish Pasty

Prep time: 25 minutes / Cook time: 20 minutes / Serves 6

Ingredients
- 150g chilled and diced butter
- 150g lard
- 600g plain flour
- 2 eggs, beaten

Filling:

- 500g beef skirt, finely chopped
- 1 small leek, finely chopped
- 200g potatoes, peeled, thinly sliced
- 180g parsnip (or swede), peeled, finely diced
- Sea salt and freshly ground black pepper, to taste
- 1/2 tsp red pepper flakes, crushed

Instructions

1. Rub the butter and lard into the flour; pour in 8 tbsp of cold water to make a firm dough. Cut your dough equally into 6 pieces and place it in your fridge for 20 minutes.
2. In the meantime, heat a large frying pan over medium-high heat. Cook the beef, leek, potatoes, and parsnip (or swede) for about 4 minutes; season with salt, black pepper, and red pepper, and reserve.
3. Roll out each piece of dough on a lightly floured working surface. Your goal is to make a disc (round) about 23cm across.
4. Firmly pack a quarter of the filling along the centre of each piece of dough. Brush the edges with the beaten egg; then, pull the pastry up and nip the top.
5. Brush on top with egg and arrange in the cooking basket.
6. Select zone 1 and pair it with "BAKE" at 180°C for 20 minutes. Select "MATCH" to duplicate settings across both zones. Press the "START/STOP" button.
7. Enjoy!

Favourite Steak & Kidney Pie

Prep time: 1 hour 15 minutes / Cook time: 45 minutes / Serves 8-9

Ingredients

Pastry:
- 500g plain flour, plus extra for rolling
- A pinch of sea salt
- 250g cold butter, cubed
- 2 medium eggs

Filling:
- 1 tbsp olive oil
- 750g beef kidney, cleaned and cut into 1-inch cubes
- 750g British top rump beef, cut into 1-inch cubes
- 100g plain flour
- 4 tbsp butter, room temperature
- 1 large carrot, trimmed and sliced
- 1 large onion, peeled and thickly chopped
- 1l off-the-boil water
- Sea salt and ground black pepper, to taste
- 1 tsp cumin powder
- 1/2 tsp dried oregano
- 1/2 tsp dried basil

- 1 large bay leaf
- 1 tbsp Worcestershire sauce

Instructions

1. To make the pastry: Blend the flour and a pinch of sea salt in your food processor. Now, fold in the butter and blend until the mixture looks like coarse breadcrumbs. Add 1 egg and 3 tbsp of water and process until a dough ball forms. Wrap the dough in cling film and leave it to rest in your fridge for about 60 minutes.
2. To make the filling: Heat the oil in a heavy frying pan over a medium-high flame. Cook the kidney and beef until no longer pink. Tip into a colander and let it drain.
3. In the same pan, melt 1 tbsp of butter over a medium-high flame. Now, saute the carrot and onion for about 7 minutes, stirring occasionally, until they've softened. Melt the remaining butter, return the meat to the pan, and coat the Ingredients with the flour.
4. Add in the remaining Ingredients and let it simmer, uncovered, for about 1½ hours, until the meat has softened and the sauce has thickened.
5. Spoon the meat/vegetable mixture into two lightly-greased pie dishes.
6. On a well-floured working surface, roll out the pastry to 5mm thick and 5cm larger than the pie dish. Carefully place the pastry over the top of the pie dish. Repeat with the other pie.
7. Make a few slashes in the lid of the pie. Whisk the egg with 2 tbsp of water to make an egg wash. Brush the surface with the egg wash and lower the pies into the cooking basket.
8. Select zone 1 and pair it with "BAKE" at 180°C for 35 minutes. Select "MATCH" to duplicate settings across both zones. Press the "START/STOP" button.
9. At the half point, turn the heat down to 20°C, and reinsert the drawers to resume cooking. Cook until golden brown and puffed.
10. Serve with a homemade potato mash, if desired.

Classic Beef Wellington

Prep time: 10 minutes / Cook time: 38 minutes / Serves 6-7

Ingredients

- 2 tbsp olive oil
- 400g brown mushrooms, chopped
- 1 large carrot, grated
- 1 medium leek, finely chopped
- 500g beef mince
- 500g pork mince
- 200ml tomato sauce

- 2 garlic cloves, finely chopped
- 2 large eggs
- Sea salt and ground black pepper, to taste
- 1 tbsp coriander, chopped
- 400g pack puff pastry

Instructions

1. Heat the olive oil in a frying pan over a medium-high flame. Sauté the mushrooms, carrots, and leek for about 3 minutes, until they are just tender; reserve.
2. In a mixing bowl, thoroughly combine the meat, tomato sauce, garlic, 1 egg, and spices. Divide the mixture into two halves and shape them into meatloaves. Lower your meatloaves into the drawers.
3. Select zone 1 and pair it with "BAKE" at 200°C for 20 minutes. Select "MATCH" to duplicate settings across both zones. Press the "START/STOP" button.
4. Meanwhile, beat the remaining egg with a little water.
5. On a lightly-floured working surface, roll the puff pastry using a rolling pin. Cut your pastry into halves.
6. Spread the sauteed vegetable mixture along the middle of the pastry. Place the prepared meatloaf on top and bring the edges together; brush with the egg wash and repeat with the other meatloaf.
7. Place Beef Wellington on the baking trays.
8. Select zone 1 and pair it with "BAKE" at 180°C for 15 minutes. Select "MATCH" to duplicate settings across both zones. Press the "START/STOP" button.
9. Enjoy!

Peppery Pilaf with Sausage

Prep time: 10 minutes / Cook time: 26 minutes / Serves 6

Ingredients

- 400g smoked sausage, casing removed and sliced
- 4 bell peppers, seeded and sliced
- 2 tsp olive oil
- 1 tsp yellow mustard
- 400g cooked white long-grain rice
- 1 small leek, sliced
- 1/2 tsp cayenne pepper
- 1/2 tsp cumin, ground
- Sea salt and ground black pepper, to taste
- 200ml chicken stock

Instructions

1. Toss smoked sausages and peppers with 1 teaspoon of olive oil. Add sausages to the zone 1 drawer. Add the peppers to the zone 2 drawer
2. Select zone 1 and pair it with "AIR FRY" at 200°C for 16 minutes. Select zone 2 and pair it with

"ROAST" at 200°C for about 15 minutes. Select "SYNC" followed by the "START/STOP" button.
3. Mix the remaining Ingredients in two baking trays; stir in the cooked sausages and peppers. Season with salt and black pepper to taste, and gently stir to combine.
4. Select zone 1 and pair it with "BAKE" at 180°C for 10 minutes. Select "MATCH" to duplicate settings across both zones. Press the "START/STOP" button.
5. Taste, adjust the seasoning, and serve immediately. Bon appétit!

Chicken Cacciatore

Prep time: 10 minutes / Cook time: 40 minutes / Serves 6

Ingredients

- 1 tbsp olive oil
- 1.5kg chicken thighs, skin-on, bone-in
- Sea salt and ground black pepper, to taste
- 300g brown (or cremini) mushrooms, sliced
- 1 onion, thinly sliced
- 2 garlic cloves, sliced
- 200ml red wine
- 400g cans tomatoes, chopped
- 200ml chicken bone broth
- 1 tsp dried oregano
- 2 bay leaves
- 2 thyme sprigs
- 2 tbsp capers
- 1 tsp red pepper flakes, crushed
- 2 tbsp black olives, pitted (optional)

Instructions

1. Rub the olive oil, salt, and black pepper over the chicken thighs.
2. Now, put them skin-side up in the drawers. Select zone 1 and pair it with "AIR FRY" at 200°C for 20 minutes. Select "MATCH" to duplicate settings across both zones. Press the "START/STOP" button.
3. Cook until crisp and golden; reserve.
4. Mix the remaining Ingredients in a large bowl. Spoon the mixture into two baking tins. Nestle the chicken back in the tins, skin-side up.
5. Select zone 1 and pair it with "BAKE" at 190°C for 20 minutes. Select "MATCH" to duplicate settings across both zones. Press the "START/STOP" button. After 10 minutes, give it a good stir, and reinsert the drawers to resume cooking.
6. Cook until the sauce is thickened and the meat is thoroughly cooked and falling off the bones.
7. Fold in the olives, if using, and serve warm. Bon appétit!

Pork Rib Hot Pot

Prep time: 2 hours / Cook time: 60 minutes / Serves 4-6

Ingredients

- 600g pork ribs, cut into individual ribs
- 1 tbsp olive oil
- 1 tsp ginger powder
- 2 tbsp apple cider vinegar
- 2 tbsp soy sauce
- 3 tbsp cornflour
- 4 garlic cloves, sliced
- 1 medium onion, peeled and sliced
- 2 bell peppers, seeded and halved
- 1 rosemary sprig
- 1 thyme sprig
- 50ml chicken stock
- 100 g smoked bacon, sliced

Instructions

1. Insert a crisper plate in both drawers. Spray the plates with nonstick cooking oil.
2. Place the pork ribs, olive oil, ginger, vinegar, and soy sauce in a ceramic dish; cover and allow it to marinate for approximately 2 hours in your fridge. Discard the marinade.
3. Toss the marinated pork ribs with cornflour and add them to the drawers.
4. Select zone 1 and pair it with "AIR FRY" at 190°C for 45 minutes. Select "MATCH" to duplicate settings across both zones. Press the "START/STOP" button.
5. At the halfway point, flip the pork ribs with silicone-tipped tongs and brush them with the reserved marinade. Reinsert drawers to resume cooking.
6. Add the other Ingredients to a lightly-greased baking tin; fold in the prepared ribs. Now, cover the baking tin with foil (shiny side down). Add the baking tin to the cooking basket.
7. Cook at 180°C for about 15 minutes. Garnish with sliced spring onions, if desired, and serve. Enjoy!

Roast Pork with Baby Carrots

Prep time: 10 minutes / Cook time: 30 minutes / Serves 4

Ingredients

- 600g pork shoulder, boneless
- 600g baby carrots, trimmed
- 1 tbsp olive oil
- Sea salt and ground black pepper, to taste
- 1 tsp red pepper flakes, crushed
- 1 tsp dried basil

Instructions

1. Pat the pork shoulder dry with tea towels. Score the rind about 1 cm deep.
2. Now, toss the pork and carrots with olive oil, salt, black pepper, red pepper, and basil.
3. Place the pork in the zone 1 drawer and the baby carrots in the zone 2 drawer.
4. Select zone 1 and pair it with "AIR FRY" at 200°C for 30 minutes. Select zone 2 and pair it with "AIR FRY" at 180°C for 20 minutes. Select "SYNC" followed by the "START/STOP" button.
5. At the halfway point, gently stir the Ingredients using a wooden spoon. Reinsert the drawers to resume cooking.
6. Let the pork rest on a carving board for about 10 minutes before slicing and serving. Serve warm pork with baby carrots.
7. Bon appétit!

British Bangers

Prep time: 20 minutes + chilling time / Cook time: 16 minutes / Serves 10

Ingredients

- 600g boneless pork shoulder, cut into small pieces
- 600g pork back fat, cut into small pieces
- 50g breadcrumbs
- Sea salt and freshly ground black pepper, to taste
- 1 tsp cayenne pepper
- 1 tbsp minced fresh sage
- 1 tsp onion powder
- 1 tsp garlic powder
- 1/2 tsp grated nutmeg
- Natural hog casing, soaked in warm water

Instructions

1. Grind the pork shoulder and fat through a medium die.
2. (Make sure your equipment is cold, or add crushed ice to the mixture). Place the mixture in the freezer for 30 minutes.
3. Ground the mixture once again, and then, test the temperature to make sure it's 1.67 °C (or colder).
4. Stir in the remaining Ingredients, except for the hog casings, and thoroughly combine the mixture with the paddle for about 4 minutes. Mix until you have a smooth mixture that can easily go into the casings!
5. Taste and adjust the seasonings. (If the meat mixture is too dry, add a little more ice water).

6. Now, fill the sausage stuffer with the mixture, and carefully stuff the sausage into hog casings. After that, twist your sausages into links.
7. If you have time, place the sausages in your fridge overnight.
8. To cook your bangers, insert a crisper plate in both drawers. Spray the plates with nonstick cooking oil.
9. Lower the sausages onto the plates. Select zone 1 and pair it with "AIR FRY" at 200°C for 16 minutes. Select "MATCH" to duplicate settings across both zones. Press the "START/STOP" button.
10. After 8 minutes, turn the bangers over, and reinsert the drawers to resume cooking.
11. Bon appétit!

Roast Beef with Banana Shallots

Prep time: 1 hour 5 minutes / Cook time: 1 hour / Serves 4

Ingredients
- 800g topside of beef
- 500g banana shallots, peeled and halved lengthways

Marinade:
- 100ml tomato sauce
- 60ml full-bodied red wine
- 1 tbsp paprika
- 1 tbsp English mustard powder
- Sea salt and ground black pepper
- 1 tbsp olive oil
- 1 tbsp redcurrant jelly

Instructions
1. In a large glass or ceramic bowl, whisk the tomato sauce, wine, paprika, mustard, salt, pepper, and olive oil. Add the beef to the marinade and let it sit for about 1 hour in your fridge.
2. Insert crisper plates into the zone 1 drawer. Spray the crisper plate with nonstick cooking oil.
3. Remove the beef from the marinade and lower it onto the crisper plate. Place banana shallots in the zone 2 drawer
4. Select zone 1 and pair it with "ROAST" at 175°C for 55 minutes to 1 hour. Select zone 2 and pair it with "AIR FRY" at 180°C for 20 minutes. Select "SYNC" followed by the "START/STOP" button.
5. At the halfway point, turn the beef over, and reinsert the drawers to resume cooking.
6. Meanwhile, cook the reserved marinade until the sauce has thickened; add the redcurrant jelly and whisk to combine well.
7. Spoon warm sauce over the roast beef and serve with air-fried banana shallots. Enjoy!

Classic Yorkies

Prep time: 10 minutes / Cook time: 20 minutes / Serves 12

Ingredients
- 1 tbsp coconut oil, room temperature
- 300g plain flour
- 1/2 tsp sea salt
- 8 medium eggs
- 500ml milk

Instructions
1. Grease Yorkshire pudding tins with coconut oil, and preheat them in your Ninja Dual Zone Air Fryer.
2. Tip plain flour into a mixing bowl along with sea salt. Beat in the eggs, followed by the milk. Continue beating until everything is well incorporated.
3. Pour the batter into a jug. Carefully and evenly pour the batter into the hot tins. Add tins to the cooking basket.
4. Select zone 1 and pair it with "BAKE" at 190°C for 20 minutes. Select "MATCH" to duplicate settings across both zones. Press the "START/STOP" button.
5. Cook until the puddings have puffed up and enjoy!

Baked Bacon Risotto

Prep time: 10 minutes / Cook time: 25 minutes / Serves 6

Ingredients
- 1 tbsp olive oil
- 200g smoked bacon, chopped
- 1 medium onion, chopped
- 2 garlic cloves, minced
- 350g risotto rice
- 50ml tomato sauce
- 600ml chicken bone broth, hot
- 1 tsp Italian spice mix
- 150g ball mozzarella, torn into chunks
- 20g breadcrumbs

Instructions
1. Thoroughly combine the olive oil, bacon, onion, and garlic in two ovenproof pans. Tip in the rice and stir to combine well. Pour over the tomato sauce and hot chicken broth. Season with Italian spice mix.
2. Cover with foil and transfer to the cooking basket.
3. Select zone 1 and pair it with "BAKE" at 190°C for 25 minutes. Select "MATCH" to duplicate settings across both zones. Press the "START/STOP" button.
4. After 15 minutes, gently stir your risotto, and add cheese and breadcrumbs to the top. Reinsert the drawers to resume cooking.

5. Bon appétit!

Homemade Soda Bread

Prep time: 10 minutes / Cook time: 35 minutes / Serves 6

Ingredients

- 350g plain wholemeal flour
- 400g plain flour
- 100g porridge oats
- 1 tsp bicarbonate of soda
- 1 tsp salt
- 30g cold butter, cut into pieces
- 750ml milk
- 1 lemon, juiced
- 1 tsp clear honey

Instructions

1. Thoroughly combine the flour, oats, soda, and salt; rub in the butter.
2. To make the buttermilk, whisk the milk with the freshly squeezed lemon juice. Gradually stir the buttermilk into the dry Ingredients. Add the honey and bring the dough together using your fingertips.
3. Tip onto a lightly floured surface. Shape the dough into two loaves and lower them onto lightly buttered baking tins.
4. Select zone 1 and pair it with "BAKE" at 200°C for 35 minutes. Select "MATCH" to duplicate settings across both zones. Press the "START/STOP" button.
5. Cool on a wire rack, then slice and serve warm.
6. Bon appétit!

Shepherd's Pie

Prep time: 10 minutes / Cook time: 37 minutes / Serves 6

Ingredients

- 1 tbsp olive oil
- 1 large carrot, chopped
- 1 large onion, chopped
- 1 large parsnip, chopped
- 500g beef mince
- 1 tbsp Worcestershire sauce
- 4 tbsp tomato purée
- 200ml vegetable broth
- 1kg potatoes, cut into chunks
- 50g butter
- 4 tbsp whole milk

Instructions

1. Heat the oil in a medium saucepan over medium-high flame; sauté the carrot, onion, and parsnip for about 3 minutes, until they've softened; reserve.
2. In the same pan, cook the beef for about 3 minutes, until no longer pink. Add the Worcestershire sauce and tomato purée.
3. Pour over 200ml broth, add the vegetables back to the pan, and spoon the mixture into an ovenproof dish.
4. Add potatoes to the zone 1 drawer; add the ovenproof dish to the zone 2 drawer.
5. Select zone 1 and pair it with "ROAST" at 190°C for 22 minutes. Select zone 2 and pair it with "AIR FRY" at 180°C for 20 minutes.
6. Select "SYNC" followed by the "START/STOP" button. At the halfway point, shake the drawer with potatoes to promote even cooking.
7. Mash the potatoes with butter and milk. Top your pie with the mash and ruffle with a fork.
8. Bake at 180°C for 15 minutes until the top is starting to colour. Enjoy!

Chicken Tikka Masala

Prep time: 10 minutes / Cook time: 20 minutes / Serves 6

Ingredients

- 2 tbsp butter, melted
- 1 sweet bell pepper, deseeded and cut into chunks
- 1 small chilli pepper, deseeded
- 3 medium shallots, halved
- 4 tbsp tikka masala paste
- 6 chicken fillets, cut into 2.5cm cubes
- 400g canned chopped tomatoes
- 50ml tomato purée
- 200ml chicken bone broth
- 2 tbsp mango chutney
- 200ml natural yoghurt
- Fresh coriander leaves, to serve (optional)
- Basmati rice, to serve (optional)

Instructions

1. Toss the peppers and shallots with 1 tablespoon of the butter and tikka masala paste. Arrange them in the zone 1 drawer.
2. Add in the chicken cubes, chopped tomatoes, tomato purée, broth, and the remaining 1 tablespoon of butter in a large casserole. Stir to combine and lower the dish into the zone 2 drawer
3. Select zone 1 and pair it with "AIR FRY" at 200°C for 15 minutes. Select zone 2 and pair it with "AIR FRY" at 200°C for about 20 minutes. Select "SYNC" followed by the "START/STOP" button.

4. At the halfway point, stir through the mango chutney and yoghurt. Afterwards, fold in the vegetables, and scatter the fresh coriander leaves. Serve with basmati rice, if desired and enjoy!

One-Pan Roast Dinner

Prep time: 10 minutes / Cook time: 30 minutes / Serves 6

Ingredients
- 800g chicken legs, skin-on, bone-in
- 2 tbsp olive oil
- 1 tbsp dried mixed herbs
- 700g potatoes, cut into roastie size
- 300g carrots, quartered
- 100ml chicken stock
- 1 tsp Marmite

Instructions
1. Pat the chicken dry with tea towels. Score the rind about 1 cm deep.
2. Toss the chicken, potatoes, and carrots with olive oil, herbs, chicken stock and Marmite.
3. Place the chicken in the zone 1 drawer and the potatoes and carrots in the zone 2 drawer.
4. Select zone 1 and pair it with "AIR FRY" at 200°C for 30 minutes. Select zone 2 and pair it with "AIR FRY" at 180°C for 25 minutes. Select "SYNC" followed by the "START/STOP" button.
5. At the halfway point, gently stir the Ingredients using a wooden spoon. Reinsert the drawers to resume cooking.
6. Let the chicken rest on a carving board for about 10 minutes before serving. Serve with potatoes with carrots.
7. Bon appétit!

Toad-in-the-Hole

Prep time: 10 minutes / Cook time: 30 minutes / Serves 4

Ingredients
- 1 tbsp olive oil
- 10 chipolatas
- Batter:
- 120g plain flour
- 1/2 tsp fine sea salt
- 2 eggs
- 160ml semi-skimmed milk

Instructions
1. Brush two baking tins with olive oil; arrange your chipolatas in the tins. Lower the tins in the cooking basket.
2. Select zone 1 and pair it with "AIR FRY" at 200°C for 15 minutes. Select "MATCH" to duplicate settings across both zones. Press the "START/STOP" button.
3. To make the batter, tip the flour into a bowl with salt. Now, create a well in the middle and crack the eggs into it.
4. Using an electric mixer, beat the mixture, gradually adding the milk. Mix to combine well.
5. Divide the batter between your tins and return them to the cooking basket.
6. Select zone 1 and pair it with "AIR FRY" at 200°C for 15 minutes. Select "MATCH" to duplicate settings across both zones. Press the "START/STOP" button.
7. Bon appétit!

Bread and Butter Pudding

Prep time: 1 hour / Cook time: 30 minutes / Serves 7-8

Ingredients
- 350ml double cream
- 300ml full-fat milk
- 1 tsp vanilla bean paste
- 3 whole eggs
- 4 tbsp golden caster sugar
- 10 slices of day-old crusty bread
- 50g butter, room temperature
- 100g dried black currants
- 2 tbsp demerara sugar

Instructions
1. In a deep saucepan, bring the cream, milk, and vanilla to a rolling boil.
2. Then, whisk the eggs and caster sugar in a jug. Slowly and gradually pour the milk mixture into the egg mixture, stirring constantly until everything is well combined.
3. Lightly butter two ovenproof dishes. Butter both sides of the bread and cut them into triangles.
4. Place half of the bread slices in the bottom of the dish. Now, sprinkle 50g of black currants over the bread. Layer the rest of the bread slices, followed by the remaining currants.
5. Pour the custard over the pudding and leave it to soak for about 1 hour in your fridge.
6. Select zone 1 and pair it with "BAKE" at 200°C for 30 minutes. Select "MATCH" to duplicate settings across both zones. Press the "START/STOP" button.
7. At the halfway point, sprinkle over the demerara sugar. Reinsert the drawers to resume cooking and cook until golden and puffed up. Devour!

CHAPTER 4 POULTRY

Chicken Balti

Prep time: 40 minutes / Cook time: 26 minutes / Serves 5

Ingredients
- 1kg skinless, boneless chicken breast, cut into bite-sized pieces
- 2 tbsp freshly squeezed lemon juice
- 1 tsp chilli powder
- 2 cardamom pods, split
- 1 tbsp olive oil
- 4 green onions, sliced
- 2 garlic cloves, very finely chopped
- 1 tsp fresh ginger, grated
- 1/2 tsp turmeric
- 1 tsp ground cumin
- 1 tsp garam masala
- 250ml tomato puree
- 2 bell peppers, deseeded and cut into small chunks
- 2 tbsp fresh parsley
- A large handful of fresh baby spinach

Instructions
1. Add the chicken, lemon juice, chilli powder, cardamom, green onions, garlic, and ginger in a ceramic bowl; leave to marinate for at least 30 minutes.
2. Heat the olive oil in a large frying pan. Saute the onion, garlic, and ginger for approximately 3 minutes.
3. Add the chicken and continue to cook for about 3 minutes, until it no longer looks raw. Divide the mixture between two baking tins.
4. Add the remaining Ingredients to the baking tins and lower them into the cooking basket.
5. Select zone 1 and pair it with "BAKE" at 200°C for 20 minutes. Select "MATCH" to duplicate settings across both zones. Press the "START/STOP" button.
6. Serve with warm chapatis, if you like. Enjoy!

Homemade Chicken Nuggets with Chips

Prep time: 10 minutes + marinating time / Cook time: 15 minutes / Serves 4

Ingredients
- 500g chicken thighs, cut into bite-sized pieces
- 120ml plain yoghurt
- 1 tbsp brown mustard
- 1 tsp garlic granules
- 1/2 tsp red pepper flakes, crushed
- Sea salt and ground black pepper, to taste
- 100g breadcrumbs, crushed
- 2 tsp olive oil
- 400g potatoes, peeled and cut into chips

Instructions
1. Place the chicken pieces in a ceramic (or glass) bowl; add the yoghurt, mustard, garlic granules, and red pepper flakes. Leave it to marinate in your fridge for about 3 hours.
2. Discard the marinade and season the chicken pieces with salt and black pepper.
3. Place the breadcrumbs on a plate and roll each piece of the marinated chicken onto the breadcrumbs, pressing to adhere. Brush the chicken pieces with 1 teaspoon of olive oil.
4. Toss potatoes with the remaining 1 teaspoon of olive oil and salt. Add chicken nuggets to the zone 1 drawer and the potato chips to the zone 2 drawer.
5. Select zone 1 and pair it with "AIR FRY" at 200°C for 15 minutes. Select zone 2 and pair it with "AIR FRY" at 200°C for about 12 minutes. Select "SYNC" followed by the "START/STOP" button.
6. Enjoy!

Turkey Ragù with a Twist

Prep time: 10 minutes / Cook time: 40 minutes / Serves 4

Ingredients
- 1 large celery rib, sliced
- 1 large carrot, sliced
- 1 large onion, sliced
- 2 tsp olive oil
- 500g turkey mince
- 1 tsp Italian seasoning mix
- Sea salt and ground black pepper, to taste
- 4 cloves garlic, finely diced
- 1 tbsp Marmite
- 100ml tomato purée

Instructions
1. Insert a crisper plate in the zone 1 drawer. Toss the vegetables with 1 teaspoon of olive oil. Arrange the vegetables on the crisper plate.
2. Mix turkey mince, olive oil, and Italian seasoning mix in a baking tin. Add the baking tin to the zone 2 drawer.
3. Select zone 1 and pair it with "ROAST" at 200°C for 20 minutes. Select zone 2 and pair it with

"AIR FRY" at 190°C for about 10 minutes. Select "SYNC" followed by the "START/STOP" button.

4. Spoon the vegetables and turkey into the lightly-greased baking tray and stir in the remaining Ingredients; gently stir to combine.
5. Cook your ragù at 180°C for 18 to 20 minutes, until cooked through.
6. Bon appétit!

Thanksgiving Turkey with Sweet Potatoes

Prep time: 10 minutes / Cook time: 55 minutes / Serves 4

Ingredients
- 600g turkey breast, boneless
- 2 tsp olive oil
- 1/2 tsp English mustard powder
- 1 tsp ground cumin
- 2 tbsp fresh lemon juice
- Sea salt and cayenne pepper, to taste
- 500g sweet potatoes

Instructions
1. Pat the turkey breasts dry using tea towels. Place the turkey breasts along with 1 teaspoon of olive oil, mustard powder, cumin, lemon juice, salt, and pepper in a resealable bag; shake until well coated on all sides.
2. Toss sweet potatoes with the remaining 1 teaspoon of olive oil, salt, and pepper.
3. Add turkey breasts to the zone 1 drawer and sweet potatoes to the zone 2 drawer.
4. Select zone 1 and pair it with "ROAST" at 175°C for 55 minutes. Select zone 2 and pair it with "AIR FRY" at 200°C for 20 minutes. Select "SYNC" followed by the "START/STOP" button.
5. When zone 1 time reaches 25 minutes, turn the turkey breasts over using silicone-tipped tongs. Reinsert the drawer to continue cooking.
6. When zone 2 time reaches 10 minutes, shake the drawer for a few seconds to promote even cooking. Reinsert the drawer to continue cooking.
7. Taste and adjust the seasonings. (Turkey breasts are done when internal temperature reaches 73°C).
8. Bon appétit!

Turkey Fricassee

Prep time: 10 minutes / Cook time: 55 minutes / Serves 4

Ingredients
- 800g boneless turkey, chopped into bite-sized chunks

- 40g butter
- 200g chestnut or button mushrooms, quartered
- 1 tbsp plain flour
- Sea salt and ground black pepper, to taste
- 100ml dry sherry
- 100ml chicken bone broth
- 100ml double cream
- 2 tbsp fresh chives for garnish, (optional)

Instructions
1. Pat the turkey dry using tea towels. Melt the butter in a frying pan over medium-high heat. Now, toss the mushrooms and turkey with flour, salt, and black pepper.
2. Cook the turkey and mushrooms for about 5 minutes. Splash in the sherry and let it bubble for a further minute; pour in the broth and bring it to a rapid boil.
3. Divide the mixture between two baking tins and lower them into the drawers.
4. Select zone 1 and pair it with "BAKE" at 180°C for 50 minutes. Select "MATCH" to duplicate settings across both zones. Press the "START/STOP" button.
5. When zone 1 time reaches 25 minutes, turn the turkey breasts over using silicone-tipped tongs. Fold in double cream and reinsert the drawers to continue cooking.
6. Serve with fresh chives, if desired, and enjoy!

Turkey Patties with Chips

Prep time: 10 minutes / Cook time: 20 minutes / Serves 4

Ingredients
- 600g turkey mince
- 2 garlic cloves, minced
- 1 large shallot, chopped
- 50g breadcrumbs
- 1 tsp smoked paprika
- Sea salt and ground black pepper, to taste
- 600g potatoes, peeled and cut into chips
- 1 tsp olive oil

Instructions
1. Insert a crisper plate in each drawer. Spray the crisper plates with nonstick cooking oil.
2. Thoroughly combine the turkey mince, garlic, shallot, breadcrumbs, and spices. Shape the mixture into four patties and spray them with cooking oil.
3. Toss potatoes with olive oil, salt, and pepper to taste.
4. Add burgers to the zone 1 drawer and potatoes to the zone 2 drawer.
5. Select zone 1 and pair it with "AIR FRY" at 190°C for 20 minutes. Select "MATCH" to duplicate settings across both zones. Press the "START/STOP" button.
6. When zone 1 time reaches 10 minutes, turn the

burgers over and spray them with cooking oil on the other side. Stir the chips and reinsert the drawer to continue cooking.

7. Bon appétit!

Amatriciana Turkey Traybake

Prep time: 10 minutes / Cook time: 30 minutes / Serves 4

Ingredients
- 1kg turkey thigs
- 1 tbsp English mustard powder
- 300ml tomato purée
- 1 tbsp Worcestershire sauce
- Sea salt and ground black pepper, to taste
- 2 rosemary sprigs
- 1 tsp olive oil
- 2 cloves garlic, smashed
- 1 sweet pepper, deseeded and sliced
- 1 small chilli pepper, deseeded and sliced
- 30g Guanciale, diced

Instructions
1. Brush two baking tins with nonstick oil, and then, divide the Ingredients between two baking tins. Stir to combine well.
2. Select zone 1 and pair it with "BAKE" at 170°C for 15 minutes. Select "MATCH" to duplicate settings across both zones. Press the "START/STOP" button.
3. Next, increase the temperature to 200°C and continue to cook for a further 15 minutes.
4. Enjoy!

Mustard Chicken with Brussels Sprouts

Prep time: 5 minutes / Cook time: 25 minutes / Serves 4

Ingredients
- 600g frozen chicken tenders
- 1 tbsp yellow mustard
- 2 tsp olive oil
- 1 tbsp dried oregano
- 1 tbsp dried rosemary
- 1 tsp garlic powder
- Sea salt and ground black pepper, to taste
- 1/2 tsp sweet paprika
- 600g Brussels sprouts, trimmed and halved

Instructions
1. Insert crisper plates in both drawers. Spray the crisper plates with nonstick cooking oil.
2. Toss chicken tenders with 1 teaspoon of oil, mustard, and spices. Toss Brussels sprouts with the remaining oil, salt, and black pepper.

3. Place the chicken tenders in the zone 1 drawer and the Brussels sprouts in the zone 2 drawer.
4. Select zone 1 and pair it with "AIR FRY" at 190°C for 25 minutes. Select zone 2 and pair it with "AIR FRY" at 190°C for 12 minutes. Select "SYNC" followed by the "START/STOP" button.
5. At the halfway point, press "START/PAUSE" and shake the Ingredients. Reinsert drawers to resume cooking.
6. Taste and adjust the seasonings. Serve warm chicken with Brussels sprouts on the side.
7. Bon appétit!

Chicken Fajitas with Squashed Avocado

Prep time: 10 minutes / Cook time: 20 minutes / Serves 5

Ingredients
- 1kg chicken breasts skinless, boneless, cut into strips
- 400g onions, peeled and sliced
- 400g bell peppers, deseeded and sliced
- 1 red chilli pepper, deveined and minced
- 2 tbsp olive oil
- 1 tbsp Mexican spice mix
- Sea salt and freshly ground black pepper, to taste
- 5 large tortillas
- 1 large avocado, pitted

Instructions
1. Insert crisper plates in both drawers. Spray the crisper plates with nonstick cooking oil.
2. Toss chicken breasts, onion, and peppers with olive oil and spices.
3. Place the chicken in the zone 1 drawer and the vegetables in the zone 2 drawer.
4. Select zone 1 and pair it with "AIR FRY" at 200°C for 15 minutes. Select zone 2 and pair it with "ROAST" at 200°C for 10 minutes. Select "SYNC" followed by the "START/STOP" button.
5. Transfer the chicken and vegetables to a plate and keep them warm.
6. Add tortillas to the drawers of your Ninja Dual Zone Air Fryer. Select "REHEAT" at 170°C for 5 minutes.
7. Scoop the flesh from the avocado, and divide it between warm tortillas. Top with the chicken pieces and vegetables. Roll them up and enjoy!

Chicken Souvlaki Salad

Prep time: 10 minutes / Cook time: 25 minutes / Serves 5

Ingredients
- 800g chicken breasts, boneless, cut into bite-sized pieces
- Sea salt and ground black pepper, to taste
- 1 tsp garlic granules

- 1 tbsp olive oil
- 1 large head of romaine lettuce, shredded
- 1 large cucumber, diced
- 200g cherry tomatoes, halved
- 100g cup kalamata olives, halved
- 1 medium red onion, sliced
- 4 tbsp Greek-style tzatziki

Instructions

1. Insert crisper plates in both drawers. Spray the crisper plates with nonstick cooking oil.
2. Toss the chicken breasts with salt, pepper, garlic granules, and olive oil.
3. Select zone 1 and pair it with "AIR FRY" at 180°C for 25 minutes. Select "MATCH" to duplicate settings across both zones. Press the "START/STOP" button.
4. In a large serving bowl, arrange the romaine lettuce, cucumbers, cherry tomatoes, olives, and red onion. Top with chicken and serve with tzatziki on the side.
5. Enjoy!

Tandoori Roast Chicken

Prep time: 2 hours / Cook time: 20 minutes / Serves 4

Ingredients
- 1kg chicken, boneless and skin-on
- 1 tsp olive oil
- Marinade:
- 200ml natural yoghurt
- 1 lime, freshly squeezed
- 1/2 tsp turmeric powder
- 1 tsp fresh ginger, peeled and grated
- 2 garlic cloves, crushed
- 1 tsp garam masala

Instructions

1. In a ceramic bowl, place the chicken with all the marinade Ingredients. Cover the bowl and leave to marinate in your fridge for at least 2 hours. Discard the marinade.
2. Brush the marinated chicken with olive oil and then, arrange them in the cooking basket.
3. Select zone 1 and pair it with "AIR FRY" at 180°C for 20 minutes. Select "MATCH" to duplicate settings across both zones. Press the "START/STOP" button.
4. At the halfway point, press "START/PAUSE", turn the chicken over, and brush with the reserved marinade. Reinsert drawers to resume cooking.
5. Bon appétit!

Chicken Kievs

Prep time: 5 minutes / Cook time: 24 minutes / Serves 5

Ingredients
- 1 kg chicken breasts, skinless and boneless
- 2 tbsp butter
- 2 garlic cloves, smashed
- Sea salt and ground black pepper, to taste
- 100g dried breadcrumbs
- 100g parmesan, grated

Instructions

1. Insert crisper plates in both drawers. Spray the crisper plates with nonstick cooking oil.
2. Pat the chicken dry with tea towels. In a small mixing bowl, thoroughly combine the butter, garlic, salt, and black pepper.
3. Divide the butter mixture between the breasts. Now, roll the chicken over the breadcrumbs.
4. Lower the prepared chicken breasts into the cooking basket.
5. Select zone 1 and pair it with "AIR FRY" at 190°C for 24 minutes. Select "MATCH" to duplicate settings across both zones. Press the "START/STOP" button.
6. At the halfway point, flip the chicken breasts with silicone-tipped tongs and top them with parmesan cheese. Reinsert drawers to resume cooking.
7. Garnish with fresh herbs and serve warm. Bon appétit!

Roast Turkey Breast

Prep time: 5 minutes / Cook time: 55 minutes / Serves 4

Ingredients
- 1 kg turkey breasts, skin-on, boneless, cut into four pieces
- 2 tsp butter, room temperature
- 2 tbsp English mustard powder
- 1 tsp cayenne pepper
- 1 tsp garlic powder
- 1 tsp onion powder
- Sea salt and ground black pepper, to taste

Instructions

1. Insert crisper plates in both drawers. Spray the crisper plates with nonstick cooking oil.
2. Pat turkey breasts dry with paper towels. Rub the butter, mustard, and spices over the skin using your hands to coat everything in the spice mixture. Transfer the turkey breasts to the zone 1 ad 2 drawers.
3. Select zone 1 and pair it with "ROAST" at 180°C for 55 minutes. Select "MATCH" to duplicate settings across both zones. Press the "START/STOP" button.
4. At the halfway point, turn the turkey breasts over and reinsert the drawers to resume cooking.
5. Bon appétit!

Mini Turkey Meatloaves

Prep time: 5 minutes / Cook time: 20 minutes / Serves 8

Ingredients
- 700g turkey mince
- 100g brown mushrooms, chopped
- 1 medium carrot, grated
- 40g bacon lardons
- 1 onion, chopped
- 2 garlic cloves, minced
- 1 egg, well-beaten
- 100g fresh breadcrumbs
- 150ml tomato paste
- 1 tbsp English mustard powder
- 1 tbsp golden syrup

Instructions
1. Brush 8 muffin cases with nonstick cooking oil.
2. Thoroughly combine the turkey mince, mushrooms, carrot, bacon, onion, garlic, egg, and breadcrumbs in a bowl.
3. In a separate bowl, whisk the tomato paste, mustard powder, and golden syrup; reserve.
4. Press the turkey mixture into the prepared muffin cases. Place them in both drawers.
5. Select zone 1 and pair it with "AIR FRY" at 180°C for 20 minutes. Select "MATCH" to duplicate settings across both zones. Press the "START/STOP" button.
6. When zone 1 time reaches 10 minutes, spread the tomato mixture over mini meatloaves and continue to cook until the centre of your meatloaf reaches 74°C.
7. Bon appétit!

Nacho Chicken Bake

Prep time: 5 minutes / Cook time: 45 minutes / Serves 6

Ingredients
- 800g chicken drumsticks, cut into pieces, boneless, skin-on
- 2 tsp olive oil
- Sea salt and ground black pepper, to taste
- 1 tsp smoked paprika
- 1 medium leek, finely sliced
- 2 garlic cloves, minced
- 1 large carrot, trimmed and sliced
- 100ml tomato sauce
- 50ml double cream
- 1 tbsp fresh parsley leaves, chopped
- 6 small corn tortillas, sliced into small wedges

Instructions
1. Pat the chicken dry with tea towels; then, toss the chicken with 1 teaspoon of olive oil, salt, pepper, and paprika.
2. Toss tortilla wedges with the remaining teaspoon of olive oil.
3. Place the chicken in the zone 1 drawer and the tortilla wedges in the zone 2 drawer.
4. Select zone 1 and pair it with "AIR FRY" at 200°C for 25 minutes. Select zone 2 and pair it with "BAKE" at 170°C for 6 minutes. Select "SYNC" followed by the "START/STOP" button.
5. At the halfway point, turn the chicken over to ensure even browning and toss the tortilla wedges; after that, reinsert the drawers to resume cooking.
6. Mix the other Ingredients in a lightly-greased baking tin. Stir to combine and nestle the chicken back in the tin, skin-side up.
7. Bake the chicken and vegetables at 180°C for 20 minutes, until thoroughly cooked. Top with the tortilla chips and serve warm.
8. Bon appétit!

Thai Chicken Drummers

Prep time: 5 minutes / Cook time: 25 minutes / Serves 9

Ingredients
- 9 chicken drumsticks, skin removed, the flesh slashed
- 2 tbsp sweet chilli sauce
- 2 tbsp of fresh orange juice
- 1 tsp fresh ginger, minced
- 1 garlic clove, crushed
- 1 tbsp good-quality Thai red curry paste

Instructions
1. Toss the chicken with the other Ingredients; make sure to coat them well. Lower the chicken drummers onto lightly greased crisper plates.
2. Select zone 1 and pair it with "AIR FRY" at 200°C for 25 minutes. Select "MATCH" to duplicate settings across both zones. Press the "START/STOP" button.
3. When zone 1 time reaches 13 minutes, turn the chicken drummers over to promote even cooking.
4. Then, reinsert the drawers to resume cooking; cook until the centre of your meatloaf reaches 74°C.
5. Bon appétit!

Sichuan Duck Wings

Prep time: 5 minutes / Cook time: 25 minutes / Serves 4

Ingredients
- 1 kg duck wings, boneless
- 1 tbsp sesame oil

- 1 tsp honey
- 1 tbsp soy sauce
- 20ml dry white wine
- 20ml orange juice
- 5g ginger, peeled and finely grated
- 1 tsp Chinese 5-spice powder
- Sea salt, to taste

Instructions

1. In a ceramic (or glass) bowl, toss the duck wings with the other Ingredients. Leave to marinate for at least 1 hour in the fridge. Reserve the marinade.
2. Select zone 1 and pair it with "AIR FRY" at 195°C for 25 minutes. Select "MATCH" to duplicate settings across both zones. Press the "START/STOP" button.
3. When zone 1 time reaches 15 minutes, turn the duck wings over, baste with the reserved marinade, and cook for a further 10 minutes.
4. Bon appétit!

Barbecued Duck with Pineapple

Prep time: 10 minutes / Cook time: 20 minutes / Serves 4

Ingredients

- 1 kg duck leg quarters, bone-in and skin-on
- 1 tbsp butter, melted
- Sea salt and ground black pepper, to taste
- 1/2 tsp hot chilli powder
- 10g orange marmalade
- 50ml BBQ sauce
- 1 small pineapple, quartered, peeled and cored

Instructions

1. Insert a crisper plate in the zone 1 drawer. Spray the plate with nonstick cooking oil. Brush the duck legs with butter and spices and lower them onto the crisper plate.
2. Select zone 1 and pair it with "AIR FRY" at 200°C for 20 minutes. Select zone 2 and pair it with "ROAST" at 170°C for 10 minutes. Select "SYNC" followed by the "START/STOP" button.
3. At the halfway point, turn the duck legs over and brush them with orange marmalade and BBQ sauce. Now, reinsert the drawers to resume cooking.
4. Let the duck legs rest for 10 minutes before carving. Top them with roasted pineapple and serve warm. Enjoy!

Homemade Taquitos

Prep time: 5 minutes / Cook time: 34 minutes / Serves 4

Ingredients

- 600g chicken fillets
- 2 bell peppers, deseeded and halved
- 1 tbsp olive oil
- 1 tsp chilli powder
- 1 tsp Mexican oregano
- Sea salt and ground black pepper, to taste
- 1 medium onion, peeled and sliced
- 100ml salsa verde
- 100g wensleydale cheese, crumbled
- 6 tortillas

Instructions

1. Insert crisper plates in both drawers. Spray the crisper plates with nonstick cooking oil.
2. Toss chicken fillets and bell pepper with olive oil and spices. Place the chicken fillets in the zone 1 drawer and the peppers in the zone 2 drawer.
3. Select zone 1 and pair it with "AIR FRY" at 200°C for 24 minutes. Select zone 2 and pair it with "ROAST" at 180°C for 20 minutes. Select "SYNC" followed by the "START/STOP" button.
4. At the halfway point, turn the chicken fillets and peppers over and reinsert the drawers to resume cooking.
5. Then, cut the chicken and peppers into strips and add the onion, salsa, and cheese. Divide the filling between tortillas. Roll them up and arrange your taquitos on both crisper plates. Lightly spray them with cooking oil.
6. Select zone 1 and pair it with "BAKE" at 180°C for 10 minutes. Select "MATCH" to duplicate settings across both zones. Press the "START/STOP" button.
7. Enjoy!

Warm Turkey Salad

Prep time: 10 minutes / Cook time: 55 minutes / Serves 6

Ingredients

- 800g turkey breasts, boneless and skinless
- 100g cherry tomatoes
- 2 tbsp extra-virgin olive oil
- Sea salt and ground black pepper, to taste
- 400g fresh baby spinach
- 1 red onion, sliced
- 2 tsp freshly squeezed lemon juice
- 100g pomegranate seeds

Instructions

1. Pat the turkey dry with tea towels. Now, toss the turkey and cherry tomatoes with 1 tablespoon of

olive oil, salt, and black pepper.

2. Place the turkey in the zone 1 drawer and the cherry tomatoes in the zone 2 drawer.

3. Select zone 1 and pair it with "ROAST" at 175°C for 55 minutes. Select zone 2 and pair it with "AIR FRY" at 195°C for 5 minutes. Select "SYNC" followed by the "START/STOP" button.

4. At the halfway point, turn the turkey and cherry tomatoes over and reinsert the drawers to resume cooking.

5. Cut the turkey into bite-sized pieces. Toss baby spinach and onion with the remaining 1 tablespoon of extra-virgin olive oil and lemon juice; top with the chicken pieces and cherry tomatoes.

6. Garnish your salad with pomegranate seeds and serve immediately. Enjoy!

English Style Chicken Breast with Asparagus & Broccoli

Prep time: 8 minutes / Cook time: 8 minutes / Serves 4

Ingredients
For chicken
- 4 Chicken Legs
- 4 tbsp olive oil
- 3 tbsp soy sauce
- 2 tbsp apple cider vinegar
- 50g brown sugar
- 1 tbsp Worcestershire Sauce
- 2 tbsp garlic, minced

For veg
- 24 asparagus spears
- 200g broccoli, chopped
- ¼ tsp sea salt
- ¼ tsp black pepper, grounded

Instructions
1. Preheat the ninja duel zone to 180°C for 4-5 minutes
2. Meanwhile, amalgamate all of the 'for chicken' Ingredients in a medium sized bowl
3. Submerge the chicken breast in the marinade
4. Place the chicken in the zone 1 draw, and asparagus spears/broccoli in the zone 2 draw
5. Dash salt and pepper In the zone 2 draw and give it a shake
6. Select zone 1, followed by 'bake' at 180°C for 15 minutes
7. Select zone 2, followed by 'roast' at 180°C for 8 minutes
8. Press 'SYNC' and then 'START/STOP' to initiate the cooking process
9. At the 8 minute mark of air baking, flip the chicken
10. Once the food content is cooked divide it onto 4 plates and serve

Air Fried Chicken Nuggets with Dip

Prep time: 1 minutes / Cook time: 10 minutes / Serves 8-10

Ingredients
- 1.5kg chicken nuggets, frozen
- 1 cal olive fry spray
- 150g tomato ketchup

Instructions
1. Remove the chicken nuggets from the packet and divide them amongst the zone draws of the air fryer, then spray them thoroughly
2. Pair the zones with 'AIR FRY' at 180°C for 10 minutes
3. Press 'MATCH' then 'START/STOP' to begin cooking the chicken nuggets
4. At the halfway point, shake the chicken nuggets and spray them again
5. Once cooked, take the chicken nuggets out of the dual zone and serve in a share dish with tomato ketchup

Baked Chicken Drumsticks

Prep time: 10 minutes / Cook time: 20 minutes / Serves 8

Ingredients
- 16 medium chicken drumsticks/1.775kg
- 2 tbsp olive oil
- 1½ tbsp cumin, grounded
- 1 ½ tbsp paprika
- 3 tsp dried oregano
- 2 garlic cloves, mashed
- 1 ½ tsp black pepper, grounded
- 1 Cal olive fry spray

Instructions
1. Using a sharp knife, create 3 small 1/2" incisions horizontally on the flesh of the chicken drumsticks, but ensure that you do not remove the skin
2. Place the chicken drum sticks into a large bowl and add the spices, hand rubbing them in thoroughly
3. Cover the bowl with cling film and place it in the refrigerator for 3hrs, allowing the flavours to infuse with the chicken
4. Spay the 1 cal fry spray around the barrel of your air fryer
5. Preheat the air fryer at 180°C for 5 minutes
6. Using some cooking tongs, place 8 chicken drumsticks in each draw of the dual zone
7. Pair the zone draws to 'BAKE' at 200°C for 20 minutes
8. At the 20-minute mark flip the chicken
9. Once complete, retrieve the chicken drum sticks to serve

CHAPTER 5 FISH & SEAFOOD

Cajun Shrimp with Roast Asparagus

Prep time: 5 minutes / Cook time: 6 minutes / Serves 4

Ingredients

- 500g shrimp, peeled and deveined
- 300g asparagus spears, trimmed and halved
- 2 tsp olive oil
- 1 teaspoon Cajun spice mix
- 1 small lemon, freshly juiced
- Sea salt and ground black pepper, to taste
- 50g Kalamata olives, pitted and sliced

Instructions

1. In a resealable bag, toss the shrimp and asparagus with olive oil, lemon juice, and spices.
2. Add shrimp to the zone 1 drawer; add the asparagus spears to the zone 2 drawer.
3. Select zone 1 and pair it with "AIR FRY" at 200°C for 6 minutes. Select "MATCH" to duplicate settings across both zones. Press the "START/STOP" button.
4. Taste and adjust seasonings. Arrange everything on a plate and serve immediately.
5. Bon appétit!

Tuna Steaks with Horseradish Sauce

Prep time: 5 minutes / Cook time: 12 minutes / Serves 4

Ingredients

- 500g tuna steak, cut into 4 pieces
- 1 tbsp olive oil
- 2 tbsp sherry wine
- 1 tsp garlic powder
- Sea salt and ground black pepper, to taste
- 4 tablespoons horseradish sauce

Instructions

1. Pat the fish dry with tea towels. Insert crisper plates in both drawers.
2. Toss the salmon with olive oil, wine, garlic, salt, and black pepper. Arrange the fish on the crisper plates.
3. Select zone 1 and pair it with "AIR FRY" at 200°C for 12 minutes. Select "MATCH" to duplicate settings across both zones. Press the "START/STOP" button.
4. At the halfway point, turn the steaks over and reinsert the drawers to resume cooking.

5. Serve warm tuna steaks with horseradish sauce on the side and enjoy!

Sea Scallops

Prep time: 5 minutes / Cook time: 7 minutes / Serves 4

Ingredients

- 500g jumbo sea scallops, cleaned and patted dry
- 2 tbsp dry white wine
- 2 tbsp lemon juice, freshly squeezed
- 1 tsp garlic granules
- 1 tsp dried basil
- 1 tsp dried rosemary
- Sea salt ground black pepper, to taste
- 1 tbsp olive oil
- 1 teaspoon capers, finely chopped
- Sweet chilli sauce, to serve (optional)

Instructions

1. Toss jumbo scallops with the other Ingredients, except chilli sauce, until they are well coated on all sides.
2. Insert crisper plates in both drawers and lower the prepared sea scallops onto the crisper plates.
3. Select zone 1 and pair it with "AIR FRY" at 200°C for 7 minutes. Select "MATCH" to duplicate settings across both zones. Press the "START/STOP" button.
4. At the halfway point, shake the basket to promote even cooking; reinsert the drawers to resume cooking.
5. Bon appétit!

Restaurant-Style Fish Fingers

Prep time: 5 minutes / Cook time: 13 minutes / Serves 4-5

Ingredients

- 600g salmon, skin off, pin-boned, cut into strips
- 1 large egg
- 100g plain flour
- 60g breadcrumbs
- 1/2 tsp cayenne pepper
- 1 teaspoon dried parsley flakes
- Sea salt and ground black pepper, to taste
- 1 tbsp olive oil

Instructions

1. Pat the fish dry with paper or tea towels. Insert

crisper plates in both drawers and spray them with cooking oil.

2. Prepare the breading station: Whisk the eggs and flour in a shallow bowl.

3. Add the breadcrumbs, followed by the seasonings, to a separate shallow bowl; stir to combine well.

4. Dip the fish pieces in the batter; next step, roll them over the breadcrumb mixture. Brush fish fingers with olive oil and lower them onto the crisper plates.

5. Select zone 1 and pair it with "AIR FRY" at 200°C for 13 minutes. Select "MATCH" to duplicate settings across both zones. Press the "START/STOP" button.

6. At the halfway point, turn the fish fingers over to ensure even browning; reinsert the drawers to resume cooking.

7. Serve warm and enjoy!

Crusted Fish Fillets

Prep time: 5 minutes / Cook time: 13 minutes / Serves 4

Ingredients

- 500g hake fillets (or white fish fillets of choice)
- 1 egg, beaten
- 80g oat flour
- 1 tsp Old Bay seasoning
- Sea salt and ground black pepper, to taste
- 1 tbsp olive oil

Instructions

1. Insert crisper plates in both drawers and spray them with cooking oil. Pat the fish dry using paper or tea towels.

2. In a shallow bowl, beat the egg until pale and frothy. On a separate plate, thoroughly combine the oat flour with Old Bay seasoning mix, salt, and black pepper.

3. Dip fish fillets in the egg mixture; then, coat both sides of the fillets with the spice/flour mixture, pressing to adhere.

4. Brush fish fillets with olive oil and arrange them onto the crisper plates.

5. Select zone 1 and pair it with "AIR FRY" at 200°C for 13 minutes. Select "MATCH" to duplicate settings across both zones. Press the "START/STOP" button.

6. At the halfway point, turn the fish over to ensure even browning; reinsert the drawers to resume cooking. Cook until your fish flakes easily when tested with a fork.

7. Bon appétit!

King Prawns with Green Beans

Prep time: 30 minutes / Cook time: 15 minutes / Serves 3

Ingredients

- 10 raw king prawns, peeled, tails on
- 1 lemon, juiced
- 2 tbsp soy sauce
- 1 tbsp olive oil
- 1 tbsp Cajun seasoning
- 300g green beans, trimmed
- Sea salt and ground black pepper, to taste
- 1/2 tsp paprika
- 2 tbsp sesame seeds

Instructions

1. Insert crisper plates in both drawers. Spray crisper plates with nonstick cooking oil.

2. In a ceramic dish, place king prawns, lemon juice, soy sauce, olive oil, and Cajun seasoning. Cover the dish and leave to marinate for about 30 minutes in the fridge.

3. Toss green beans with salt, black pepper, and paprika.

4. Place the king prawns in the zone 1 drawer, discarding the marinade. Place the green beans in the zone 2 drawer.

5. Select zone 1 and pair it with "AIR FRY" at 200°C for 10 minutes. Select zone 2 and pair it with "AIR FRYER" at 200°C for 15 minutes. Select "SYNC" followed by the "START/STOP" button.

6. When zone 1 time reaches 5 minutes, turn the prawns over using silicone-tipped tongs; reinsert the drawer to continue cooking.

7. When zone 2 time reaches 8 minutes, stir green beans to promote even cooking; reinsert the drawer to continue cooking.

8. Sprinkle green beans with sesame seeds and serve with king prawns. Enjoy!

Roast Fish with Vegetables

Prep time: 10 minutes / Cook time: 20 minutes / Serves 4

Ingredients

- 600g cod fillets
- 1 tbsp dried sage
- 1 tbsp dried rosemary
- 2 garlic cloves
- Sea salt and ground black pepper, to taste
- 200g cherry tomatoes
- 2 bell peppers, deveined and halved
- 2 tsp olive oil

Instructions

1. Insert crisper plates in both drawers. Spray crisper plates with nonstick cooking oil.
2. Pat the fish fillets dry using paper towels. Crush the sage, rosemary, and garlic in a pestle and mortar.
3. Coat fish fillets with crushed herbs, salt, and pepper. Toss cherry tomatoes and peppers with salt and pepper.
4. Brush the fish and vegetables with olive oil. Add the cod fillets to the zone 1 drawer and the vegetables to the zone 2 drawer.
5. Select zone 1 and pair it with "ROAST" at 200°C for 20 minutes. Select zone 2 and pair it with "AIR FRYER" at 200°C for 15 minutes. Select "SYNC" followed by the "START/STOP" button.
6. When zone 1 time reaches 10 minutes, turn the fish fillets over to ensure even cooking. Reinsert the drawer to continue cooking.
7. When zone 2 time reaches 7 minutes, remove cherry tomatoes from the cooking basket; reinsert the drawer to continue cooking.
8. Serve with lemon slices and enjoy!

Baked Piri-Piri Tilapia with Squash

Prep time: 10 minutes / Cook time: 20 minutes / Serves 4

Ingredients

- 600g tilapia
- 300g squash, peeled and cut into 1cm chunks
- Sea salt and cayenne pepper, to taste
- Piri-Piri Sauce:
- 4 hot pickled peppers
- 2 garlic cloves
- Fresh juice and zest 1 lemon
- 2 tbsp extra-virgin olive oil
- 1 tbsp smoked paprika

Instructions

1. Pat the fish dry using paper towels. Grease two baking tins with nonstick cooking oil.
2. Blend the sauce Ingredients in your food processor until fine; reserve. Toss the fish and squash with salt and cayenne pepper to taste.
3. Add the tilapia fillets to the zone 1 drawer and the squash to the zone 2 drawer.
4. Select zone 1 and pair it with "BAKE" at 200°C for 20 minutes. Select zone 2 and pair it with "BAKE" at 200°C for 12 minutes. Select "SYNC" followed by the "START/STOP" button.
5. When zone 1 time reaches 10 minutes, turn the fish over and top it with the prepared piri-piri sauce.

Reinsert the drawer to continue cooking.
6. When zone 2 time reaches 6 minutes, toss the squash chunks and reinsert the drawer to continue cooking.
7. Bon appétit!

Halibut Parcels

Prep time: 10 minutes / Cook time: 15 minutes / Serves 6

Ingredients

- 6 (about 120g each) halibut steaks
- 2 tsp olive oil
- 3 bell peppers, sliced
- 2 tbsp soy sauce
- 1 tbsp Old Bay spice mix
- 2 garlic cloves, chopped
- 6 small spring onions, chopped
- 6 slices lemon

Instructions

1. Insert crisper plates in both drawers. Then, cut out 6 squares of foil with scissors (each about 30cm). Brush pieces of foil with olive oil.
2. Toss halibut steaks and peppers with soy sauce and Old Bay spice mix.
3. Divide halibut steaks, peppers, garlic, and spring onions between the prepared foil pieces.
4. Then, fold over the edges of the foil to seal. Lay the halibut parcels onto the crisper plates.
5. Select zone 1 and pair it with "AIR FRY" at 200°C for 15 minutes. Select "MATCH" to duplicate settings across both zones. Press the "START/STOP" button.
6. When zone 1 time reaches 8 minutes, open the foil. Reinsert the drawers to continue cooking.
7. Garnish each parcel with a lemon slice and enjoy!

Fish Pie Mac 'n' Cheese

Prep time: 5 minutes / Cook time: 25 minutes / Serves 6

Ingredients

- 1 tbsp olive oil
- 400g pasta of choice
- 650ml milk
- 50g plain flour
- 40g butter
- 600g fish pie mix (smoked fish and white)
- 150g mature cheddar, grated

Instructions

1. Remove a crisper plate from your Ninja Dual Zone Air Fryer. Brush two baking tins with olive oil.

2. Cook pasta according to the manufacturer's Instructions, until just cooked; drain.
3. In a large saucepan, cook the milk along with the flour and butter over medium flame. Whisk it continuously until you have a smooth sauce. Heat off.
4. Tip the pasta into the sauce; gently stir to combine.
5. Add fish to the prepared baking tins and spoon the pasta/sauce mixture over the top.
6. Select zone 1 and pair it with "BAKE" at 180°C for 25 minutes. Select "MATCH" followed by the "START/STOP" button.
7. When zone 1 time reaches 10 minutes, turn the fish fillets over and then scatter them with cheddar cheese. Bake until golden and reinsert the drawer to continue cooking.
8. Bon appétit!

Tiger Prawns with Courgette

Prep time: 5 minutes / Cook time: 12 minutes / Serves 4-5

Ingredients
- 1kg tiger prawns, peeled, tails on
- 1 tbsp olive oil
- 2 tbsp fresh lemon juice
- 1 tbsp stone-ground mustard
- 1 tsp dried parsley flakes
- 1/2 tsp onion powder
- 1 tsp garlic granules
- 1/4 tsp ground cumin
- Sea salt and ground black pepper, to taste
- 500g courgette, sliced

Instructions
1. Insert crisper plates in both drawers. Spray the crisper plates with nonstick cooking oil.
2. Toss tiger prawns with olive oil, lemon juice, mustard, and spices. Toss courgette slices with salt, black pepper, and olive oil.
3. Place the prawns in the zone 1 drawer and the courgette slices in the zone 2 drawer.
4. Select zone 1 and pair it with "AIR FRY" at 200°C for 5 minutes. Select zone 2 and pair it with "AIR FRY" at 200°C for 12 minutes. Select "SYNC" followed by the "START/STOP" button.
5. Bon appétit!

Fish and Mushroom Patties

Prep time: 10 minutes / Cook time: 20 minutes / Serves 4-5

Ingredients
- 1kg white fish fillets, boneless and flaked
- 200g brown mushrooms, chopped
- 2 garlic cloves, pressed
- 1 small leek, chopped
- 2 slices of stale bread, crustless
- 1 large egg, beaten
- 2 tbsp fresh cilantro leaves, finely chopped
- Sea salt and ground black pepper, to taste
- 1 tsp smoked paprika
- 100g dried breadcrumbs

Instructions
1. Insert crisper plates in both drawers. Line the crisper plates with baking parchment.
2. In a mixing bowl, thoroughly combine the fish, mushrooms, garlic, leek, bread, egg, cilantro, salt, black pepper, and smoked paprika.
3. Mix to combine well and roll the fish mixture into 4-5 patties.
4. Place dried breadcrumbs in a shallow dish; then, roll the fish patties over the breadcrumbs, pressing to adhere well; arrange fish patties on the prepared crisper plates.
5. Select zone 1 and pair it with "AIR FRY" at 200°C for 20 minutes. Select "MATCH" to duplicate settings across both zones. Press the "START/STOP" button.
6. When zone 1 time reaches 10 minutes, turn the fish patties over to ensure even cooking. Reinsert the drawers to continue cooking.
7. Bon appétit!

Sea Scallop Salad

Prep time: 10 minutes / Cook time: 15 minutes / Serves 4-5

Ingredients
- 500g sea scallops, cleaned and patted dry
- 2 bell peppers, deseeded and halved
- 1 medium courgette, sliced
- 1 tsp garlic granules
- 1 tsp dried Italian spice mix
- Sea salt ground black pepper, to taste
- 2 tbsp dry white wine
- 2 tbsp lemon juice, freshly squeezed
- 2 tsp olive oil
- 1 small onion, thinly sliced
- 50g black olives, pitted and sliced

Instructions
1. Insert crisper plates in both drawers Toss jumbo scallops with the spices, wine, lemon juice, and 1 teaspoon of olive oil; toss until they are well coated on all sides.

2. Toss bell peppers and courgettes with the remaining 1 teaspoon of olive oil, salt, and black pepper.
3. Add the sea scallops to the zone 1 drawer and the vegetables to the zone 2 drawer.
4. Select zone 1 and pair it with "AIR FRY" at 200°C for 7 minutes. Select zone 2 and pair it with "AIR FRY" at 200°C for 15 minutes. Select "SYNC" followed by the "START/STOP" button.
5. At the halfway point, shake the basket to promote even cooking; reinsert the drawers to resume cooking.
6. Add sea scallops and vegetables to a salad bowl. Add the onions and olives, and toss to combine well.
7. Taste, adjust the seasoning, and serve immediately. Bon appétit!

Classic Fish Mappas

Prep time: 5 minutes / Cook time: 21 minutes / Serves 5

Ingredients
- 400g basmati rice
- 1 tbsp olive oil
- 1 large onion, sliced
- 2 garlic cloves, chopped
- 2 tbsp tikka curry paste
- 2 medium tomatoes, chopped
- 1kg white fish fillets, cut into bite-sized chunks
- 200ml canned coconut milk

Instructions
1. Remove a crisper plate from your Ninja Dual Zone Air Fryer. Spray two baking tins with cooking oil.
2. Cook the rice according to the pack Instructions; fluff the rice with a fork and divide it between the prepared baking tins.
3. Meanwhile, heat the oil in a saucepan over moderately high heat. Saute the onion and garlic for about 3 minutes, stirring frequently.
4. Add the curry paste and tomatoes. Now, add the sauteed mixture to the baking tins. Add the fish to the tins.
5. Select zone 1 and pair it with "AIR FRY" at 180°C for 18 minutes. Select "MATCH" to duplicate settings across both zones. Press the "START/STOP" button.
6. When zone 1 time reaches 9 minutes, add canned coconut milk to the rice mixture and gently stir to combine. Reinsert the drawers to continue cooking. Enjoy!

Cod Fish Croquettes

Prep time: 10 minutes / Cook time: 14 minutes / Serves 4

Ingredients
- 800g cod fish fillets, flaked
- 1 large egg, beaten
- 2 tbsp milk
- 1 large slice of white bread, crustless
- 2 green onions, chopped
- 2 garlic cloves, pressed
- 2 tbsp fresh parsley leaves, finely chopped
- 1 tsp cayenne pepper
- 100g crushed tortilla chips
- Sea salt and ground black pepper, to taste

Instructions
1. Insert crisper plates in both drawers. Line the crisper plates with baking parchment.
2. In a mixing bowl, combine all the Ingredients until everything is well incorporated.
3. Roll the mixture into small patties and arrange them on the prepared crisper plates.
4. Select zone 1 and pair it with "AIR FRY" at 200°C for 14 minutes. Select "MATCH" to duplicate settings across both zones. Press the "START/STOP" button.
5. When zone 1 time reaches 7 minutes, turn the croquettes over to promote even cooking. Reinsert the drawers to continue cooking.
6. Serve warm croquettes with a fresh salad of choice. Bon appétit!

Prawn and Green Bean Salad

Prep time: 10 minutes / Cook time: 12 minutes / Serves 4

Ingredients
- 9 raw prawns, peeled, tails on
- 400g green beans, trimmed
- 1/2 tsp paprika, or more to taste
- 1/2 tsp dried oregano
- 1/2 tsp dried basil
- Sea salt and ground black pepper, to taste
- 1 red onion, sliced into rings
- 1 bell pepper, deseeded and sliced
- 200g cherry tomatoes, halved
- 1 tbsp balsamic vinegar
- 1 medium lemon, juiced

Instructions
1. Insert crisper plates in both drawers. Spray crisper plates with nonstick cooking oil.
2. Toss the prawns with paprika, oregano, basil, salt, and black pepper. Toss green beans with salt and black pepper. Spray the Ingredients with cooking oil.

3. Place the prawns in the zone 1 drawer and the green beans in the zone 2 drawer.
4. Select zone 1 and pair it with "AIR FRY" at 200°C for 12 minutes. Select zone 2 and pair it with "ROAST" at 200°C for 10 minutes. Select "SYNC" followed by the "START/STOP" button.
5. At the halfway point, shake the basket to promote even cooking; reinsert the drawers to resume cooking.
6. Toss the prawns and green beans with the other Ingredients and serve immediately. Enjoy!

Tilapia with Asparagus

Prep time: 10 minutes / Cook time: 20 minutes / Serves 4

Ingredients
- 600g tilapia fillets
- 1 tbsp tandoori paste
- Sea salt and ground black pepper, to taste
- 300g asparagus spears, trimmed and sliced into 2.5cm pieces
- 2 tsp olive oil
- 1 red chilli pepper, deseeded and chopped

Instructions
1. Insert crisper plates in both drawers. Spray crisper plates with nonstick cooking oil.
2. Pat the fish fillets dry using paper towels. Coat fish fillets with tandoori paste, salt, and pepper. Toss the asparagus spears with salt and pepper.
3. Brush the fish and asparagus spears with olive oil. Add the fish fillets to the zone 1 drawer and the asparagus spears to the zone 2 drawer.
4. Select zone 1 and pair it with "AIR FRY" at 200°C for 20 minutes. Select zone 2 and pair it with "AIR FRYER" at 200°C for 6 minutes. Select "SYNC" followed by the "START/STOP" button.
5. When zone 1 time reaches 10 minutes, turn the fish fillets over to ensure even cooking. Reinsert the drawer to continue cooking.
6. When zone 2 time reaches 7 minutes, toss the asparagus and reinsert the drawer to continue cooking.
7. Serve with chilli pepper and enjoy!

Easy Homemade Calamari

Prep time: 1 hour 5 minutes / Cook time: 10 minutes / Serves 5

Ingredients
- 600g squid, cleaned and cut into rings
- 2 tbsp soy sauce
- 100ml stout
- 1 tsp garlic granules
- 1 tbsp English mustard powder
- 1/2 tsp ground cumin
- Sea salt and ground black pepper, to your liking
- 120g all-purpose flour
- 1 large egg
- 120g breadcrumbs
- 2 tsp olive oil

Instructions
1. Insert crisper plates in both drawers and spray them with cooking oil.
2. Toss the squid with soy sauce, stout, and spices. Cover and let it marinate in your fridge for about 1 hour. Discard the marinade.
3. Place the flour in a shallow dish. In a separate dish, whisk the egg until pale and frothy. Add the breadcrumbs to a third shallow dish.
4. Dust the calamari rings in the flour. Then, dip them into the egg mixture; finally, coat them with the breadcrumbs, pressing them to adhere on all sides. Drizzle the calamari rings with olive oil.
5. Place calamari onto crisper plates. Select zone 1 and pair it with "AIR FRY" at 200°C for 10 minutes. Select "MATCH" to duplicate settings across both zones. Press the "START/STOP" button.
6. Shake the drawers halfway through the cooking time. Serve calamari with your favourite sauce on the side. Enjoy!

Seafood Pilaf with Coriander Chutney

Prep time: 10 minutes / Cook time: 20 minutes / Serves 6

Ingredients
- 300g cod fish, skinless, boneless and cut into strips
- 300g shrimp, cleaned and deveined
- 1 tbsp olive oil
- 2 bell peppers, deveined and chopped
- 200ml fish stock
- 200g can tomatoes, chopped
- 1 onion, chopped
- 2 garlic cloves, crushed or finely chopped
- 300g cooked rice
- 50g cashews, soaked overnight
- 1 tbsp grated ginger
- 1 green chilli, sliced
- 2 garlic cloves, crushed
- 2 tsp coriander seeds, crushed

Instructions

1. In a large bowl; thoroughly combine the fish, shrimp, olive oil, peppers, fish stock, tomatoes, onion, garlic, and rice. Divide the mixture between two baking tins. Add baking tins to the drawers.
2. Select zone 1 and pair it with "ROAST" at 180°C for 20 minutes. Select "MATCH" to duplicate settings across both zones. Press the "START/STOP" button.
3. At the halfway point, stir your pilaf with a wooden spoon and reinsert the drawers to resume cooking.
4. In a high-speed blender, process the cashews, ginger, green chilli, garlic, and coriander seeds with 50ml water. Blend the Ingredients until you have a spoonable sauce.
5. When your pilaf is ready, fluff up the grains with a fork. Spoon over the coriander chutney and serve warm. Bon appétit!

Halibut & Dill Fish Cakes

Prep time: 10 minutes / Cook time: 25 minutes / Serves 6

Ingredients

- 600g Maris Piper potato, peeled and diced
- 600g halibut, skinless and flaked
- A small bunch of dill, stalks and fronds separated, chopped
- 1 tbsp lemon juice
- 4 tbsp mayonnaise
- 4 tbsp caper, rinsed
- Sea salt and ground black pepper, to taste
- 1 egg, beaten
- 100g breadcrumb
- 1 tbsp oil

Instructions

1. Insert a crisper plate in each drawer. Spray the crisper plates with nonstick cooking oil.
2. Cook the potatoes in boiling salted water for about 10 minutes, or until fork-tender. Drain well and mash the potatoes with a fork.
3. Stir in the halibut, dill, lemon juice, mayonnaise, caper, salt, and black pepper.
4. Dip the cakes into the beaten egg, then press into the breadcrumbs all over. Arrange fish cakes on the drawers.
5. Select zone 1 and pair it with "AIR FRY" at 200°C for 15 minutes. Select "MATCH" to duplicate settings across both zones. Press the "START/STOP" button.
6. When zone 1 time reaches 10 minutes, turn the fish cakes over and reinsert the drawer to continue cooking.
7. Bon appétit!

Crispy Prawns

Prep time: 5 minutes / Cook time: 7 minutes / Serves 2

Ingredients

- 150 g prawns
- 175 g breadcrumbs
- 1 egg beaten
- 30 g parmesan cheese
- 1 tsp smoked paprika
- Spray oil

Instructions

1. Mix breadcrumbs, parmesan and paprika in a bowl.
2. Bread prawns by first dipping prawn into beaten egg and then breadcrumb mixture.
3. Arrange prawns in airfryer basket and spray with spray oil#
4. Cook for about 6-8 minutes at 180°C.

Tiger Prawns with Courgettes

Prep time: 10 minutes / Cook time: 18 minutes / Serves 4

Ingredients

- 16 large tiger prawns, peeled, tails on
- 2 tbsp dry white wine
- 1 medium lemon, zested and juiced
- 1 tbsp Dijon mustard
- Sea salt and ground black pepper, to your liking
- 1 tsp garlic granules
- 1 tsp dried parsley flakes
- 500g courgettes, cut in 2.5cm pieces

Instructions

1. Insert a crisper plate into zone 1. Spray the crisper plate with nonstick cooking oil.
2. Toss tiger prawns with wine, lemon, mustard, salt, black pepper, garlic, and parsley flakes.
3. Toss courgette pieces with salt and black pepper to your liking.
4. Place the prawns in the zone 1 drawer. Place the courgette in the zone 2 drawer (with no crisper plate inserted).
5. Select zone 1 and pair it with "AIR FRY" at 200°C for 9 to 10 minutes. Select zone 2 and pair it with "ROAST" at 200°C for 16 to 18 minutes. Select "SYNC" followed by the "START/STOP" button.
6. When zone 1 time reaches 5 minutes, turn the prawns over using silicone-tipped tongs.
7. Serve immediately and enjoy!

CHAPTER 6 BEEF, PORK & LAMB

Bangers and Mash

Prep time: 5 minutes / Cook time: 20 minutes / Serves 6

Ingredients
- 2 tsp olive oil
- 6 pork sausages (the best quality you can find)
- 800kg King Edward potatoes, peeled and cut into 2.5cm chunks
- 40ml milk
- 40ml double cream
- 20g butter, diced
- A pinch of grated nutmeg
- Sea salt and ground black pepper, to taste

Instructions
1. Toss pork sausages with 1 tsp of olive oil. Toss potatoes wth the remaining teaspoon of olive oil, salt, and pepper.
2. Add sausages to the zone 1 drawer; add the potatoes to the zone 2 drawer.
3. Select zone 1 and pair it with "AIR FRY" at 190°C for 15 minutes. Select zone 2 and pair it with "AIR FRY" at 200°C for 20 minutes. Select "SYNC" followed by the "START/STOP" button.
4. At the halfway point, shake the drawers to promote even cooking.
5. Mash your potatoes with the milk, cream, and butter.
6. To serve, scoop a big mound of mash onto the middle of each plate, then top with the sausages and enjoy!

Traditional Scouse

Prep time: 5 minutes / Cook time: 40 minutes / Serves 6

Ingredients
- 1 tbsp olive oil
- 800g lamb neck fillet, cut into chunky pieces
- 1 tbsp plain flour
- Sea salt and ground black pepper, to taste
- 1 large onion, chopped
- 150ml chicken broth
- 2 carrots, cut into chunks
- 300g turnip, cut into chunks
- 150ml bitter ale
- 2 thyme sprigs

Instructions
1. Heat olive oil in a frying pan over medium-high heat. Now, toss the meat with flour, salt, and black pepper.
2. Cook the meat and onion for about 5 minutes. Splash in the chicken broth and bring it to a rapid boil. Add the remaining Ingredients, except the ale, and stir to combine.
3. Divide the mixture between two baking tins and lower them into the drawers.
4. Select zone 1 and pair it with "BAKE" at 180°C for 40 minutes. Select "MATCH" to duplicate settings across both zones. Press the "START/STOP" button.
5. When zone 1 time reaches 20 minutes, pour in ale and reinsert the drawers to continue cooking.
6. Bon appétit!

Bacon Butties

Prep time: 5 minutes / Cook time: 10 minutes / Serves 6

Ingredients
- 8 rashers rindless back bacon
- 1 large onion, sliced into rings
- 1 bread loaf
- 2 tsp butter
- 4 tbsp tomato chutney

Instructions
1. Insert a crisper plate in the zone 1 and 2 drawers.
2. Add the bacon to the zone 1 drawer and the onion to the zone 2 drawer.
3. Select zone 1 and pair it with "AIR FRY" at 200°C for 10 minutes. Select zone 2 and pair it with "AIR FRY" at 180°C for 9 minutes.
4. Select "SYNC" followed by the "START/STOP" button. At the halfway point, turn the bacon rashers and onion rings with silicone-tipped tongs to promote even cooking.
5. Cut 8 slices from the loaf and butter each one on one side. Spread the chutney evenly over 4 slices of the bread and top each with 2 rashers of bacon. Top with the other slices of bread and press together to form the butties.
6. Bake the butties at 180°C for 6 minutes. Cut the butties in half and enjoy!

Lamb Chops with Broccoli

Prep time: 10 minutes / Cook time: 12 minutes / Serves 3

Ingredients

- 3 lamb loin chops, 2.5cm thick
- 200g plain flour
- 1 tsp chilli powder
- 1 tsp garlic granules
- Sea salt and ground black pepper, to taste
- 2 eggs
- 500g broccoli, broken into 2.5cm florets
- 2 tsp sunflower oil

Instructions

1. Pat the lamb loin chops dry with tea towels.
2. Thoroughly combine the flour, chilli powder, garlic granules, salt, and black pepper.
3. Beat the eggs until pale and frothy. Dip the chops in the beaten egg, then in the flour mixture; repeat the process one more time, ending with the flour. Set them aside.
4. Place the lamb loin chops in the zone 1 drawer and brush them with 1 teaspoon of oil. Toss broccoli florets with the remaining teaspoon of oil and place them in the zone 2 drawer.
5. Select zone 1 and pair it with "AIR FRY" at 200°C for 12 minutes. Select zone 2 and pair it with "ROAST" at 190°C for 9 minutes. Select "SYNC" followed by the "START/STOP" button.
6. When zone 1 time reaches 6 minutes, turn the lamb loin chops over using silicone-tipped tongs. Reinsert the drawer to continue cooking.
7. When zone 2 time reaches 5 minutes, shake the drawer to ensure even browning. Reinsert the drawer to continue cooking.
8. Bon appétit!

Pork Loin Steaks with Baby Carrots

Prep time: 10 minutes / Cook time: 20 minutes / Serves 4

Ingredients

- 600g pork loin steaks
- 500g baby carrots, cut in half, stem removed
- 2 tsp butter, melted
- 1 tbsp hot paprika
- 1/2 tsp garlic granules
- Sea salt and ground black pepper, to taste

Instructions

1. Insert a crisper plate in the zone 1 drawer. Spray the crisper plate with nonstick cooking oil.
2. Toss pork loin steaks and baby carrots with melted butter, paprika, garlic granules, salt, and black pepper.
3. Place the pork loin steaks in the zone 1 drawer. Place baby carrots in the zone 2 drawer (with no crisper plate inserted).
4. Select zone 1 and pair it with "AIR FRY" at 185°C for 20 minutes. Select zone 2 and pair it with "ROAST" at 180°C for 15 minutes. Select "SYNC" followed by the "START/STOP" button. Enjoy!

Pork Medallions with Roasted Peppers

Prep time: 10 minutes / Cook time: 30 minutes / Serves 4

Ingredients

- 600g pork medallions
- 1 tbsp butter, melted
- 1/2 tsp garlic granules
- 1/2 tsp onion powder
- 1 tbsp cayenne pepper
- 1 tsp English mustard powder
- 4 bell peppers, cut in half, deseeded
- 1 tsp sunflower oil
- Sea salt and ground black pepper, to taste

Instructions

1. Insert a crisper plate in the zone 1 drawer. Spray the crisper plate with nonstick cooking oil.
2. Toss pork medallions with melted butter, garlic granules, onion powder, cayenne pepper, mustard powder, salt, and black pepper. Toss bell peppers with oil, salt, and black pepper.
3. Place the pork medallions in the zone 1 drawer. Place bell peppers in the zone 2 drawer (with no crisper plate inserted).
4. Select zone 1 and pair it with "AIR FRY" at 190°C for 30 minutes. Select zone 2 and pair it with "ROAST" at 200°C for 15 minutes. Select "SYNC" followed by the "START/STOP" button. Enjoy!

Gammon Steaks with Butternut Squash

Prep time: 5 minutes / Cook time: 20 minutes / Serves 2

Ingredients

- 2 (150g each) gammon steaks
- 1 tsp dried basil
- 1 tsp English mustard powder

- 1/2 tsp onion powder
- 1/2 tsp garlic granules
- 1 tsp dried sage
- Sea salt and ground black pepper, to taste
- 300g butternut squash, peeled and cut into 1.5cm chunks
- 2 tsp vegetable oil

Instructions

1. Insert a crisper plate into the zone 1 drawer. Spray the crisper plate with nonstick cooking oil.
2. Toss gammon steaks with basil, mustard powder, onion powder, garlic granules, sage, salt, and black pepper. Brush gammon steaks with 1 teaspoon of vegetable oil.
3. Toss the butternut squash with salt, pepper, and the remaining 1 teaspoon of vegetable oil.
4. Place gammon steaks in the zone 1 drawer. Place the butternut squash in the zone 2 drawer (with no crisper plate inserted).
5. Select zone 1 and pair it with "AIR FRY" at 180°C for 20 minutes. Select zone 2 and pair it with "ROAST" at 200°C for 12 minutes. Select "SYNC" followed by the "START/STOP" button.
6. Bon appétit!

Fillet Steak with Chilli Squash

Prep time: 1 hour / Cook time: 25 minutes / Serves 4

Ingredients
- 500g beef fillet steak, sliced
- 1 tbsp English mustard
- 2 tbsp soy sauce
- 50ml dry red wine
- 1/2 tsp onion powder
- 1 tsp dried rosemary, crushed
- Sea salt and ground black pepper, to taste
- 300g butternut squash, peeled and cut into 1.5cm chunks
- 1 tsp chilli powder
- 2 tsp vegetable oil

Instructions

1. In a ceramic bowl, place the beef, mustard, soy sauce, wine, onion powder, rosemary, salt, and black pepper. Allow it to marinate for at least 1 hour.
2. Toss the butternut squash with salt, pepper, chilli powder, and 1 teaspoon of vegetable oil.
3. Place fillet steaks in the zone 1 drawer and brush them with 1 teaspoon of vegetable oil. Place the butternut squash in the zone 2 drawer.
4. Select zone 1 and pair it with "ROAST" at 200°C for

25 minutes. Select zone 2 and pair it with "ROAST" at 200°C for 12 minutes. Select "SYNC" followed by the "START/STOP" button.
5. At the halfway point, shake the basket to promote even cooking; reinsert the drawers to resume cooking.
6. Bon appétit!

Homemade Burgers with Sweet Potato Chips

Prep time: 10 minutes / Cook time: 20 minutes / Serves 4

Ingredients
- 500g beef mince
- 1 large shallot, chopped
- 2 garlic cloves, minced
- 50g tortilla chips, crushed
- 2 tbsp BBQ sauce
- Sea salt and ground black pepper, to taste
- 600g sweet potatoes, peeled and cut into chips
- 2 tsp olive oil

Instructions

1. Insert a crisper plate in each drawer. Spray the crisper plates with nonstick cooking oil.
2. Thoroughly combine the beef mince, shallot, garlic, tortilla chips, BBQ sauce, salt, and black pepper. Shape the mixture into four patties and brush them with 1 teaspoon of olive oil.
3. Toss potatoes with the remaining teaspoon of olive oil, salt, and black pepper.
4. Add burgers to the zone 1 drawer and sweet potatoes to the zone 2 drawer.
5. Select zone 1 and pair it with "AIR FRY" at 190°C for 20 minutes. Select "MATCH" to duplicate settings across both zones. Press the "START/STOP" button.
6. When zone 1 time reaches 10 minutes, turn the burgers and chips over to promote even cooking; reinsert the drawers to resume cooking.
7. Bon appétit!

Next Level Beef with Roasted Tomatoes

Prep time: 2 hours / Cook time: 18 minutes / Serves 4

Ingredients
- 1 tbsp dried sage
- 1 tbsp fried rosemary
- 1 tbsp dried thyme
- 1 large garlic clove
- 1 small knob of fresh ginger, peeled
- 600g beef shin, cut into large chunks
- 1 tsp brown miso paste

- 100ml sweet brown ale
- Sea salt and ground black pepper, to taste
- 400g cherry tomatoes
- 2 tsp olive oil

Instructions

1. Insert a crisper plate into the zone 1 drawer. Spray the crisper plate with nonstick cooking oil.
2. Crush the herbs, garlic, and ginger in a pestle and mortar. Add beef shin, miso paste, and brown ale to a ceramic (or glass) bowl; add in the crushed aromatics, cover, and leave to marinate in your fridge for at least 2 hours.
3. Season the beef with salt and pepper, and brush it with 1 teaspoon of olive oil. Toss cherry tomatoes with the remaining 1 teaspoon of olive oil, salt, and black pepper.
4. Place the beef shin in the zone 1 drawer. Place the tomatoes in the zone 2 drawer (with no crisper plate inserted).
5. Select zone 1 and pair it with "AIR FRY" at 200°C for 18 minutes. Select zone 2 and pair it with "ROAST" at 200°C for 10 minutes. Select "SYNC" followed by the "START/STOP" button.
6. At the halfway point, shake your food or toss it with silicone-tipped tongs to promote even cooking. Enjoy!

Rarebit Pork Loin Steaks

Prep time: 5 minutes / Cook time: 20 minutes / Serves 4

Ingredients
- 4 pork loin steaks
- 1 tbsp olive oil
- 2 tsp wholegrain mustard
- 1 tsp garlic granules
- Sea salt and ground black pepper, to taste
- A pinch of grated nutmeg
- 100g mature cheddar, grated
- 2 tbsp double cream

Instructions
1. Pat the pork loin steaks dry with kitchen towels. Place the pork loin steaks in two roasting trays and lower them into the cooking basket. Brush them with olive oil.
2. Select zone 1 and pair it with "AIR FRY" at 200°C for 20 minutes. Select "MATCH" to duplicate settings across both zones. Press the "START/STOP" button.
3. In the meantime, thoroughly combine the mustard, spices, cheddar, and double cream. When zone 1 time reaches 10 minutes, spread over the top of the pork loin steaks.
4. Reinsert the drawers to continue cooking. Bon appétit!

Rib-Eye Steaks with Chilli Butter

Prep time: 5 minutes / Cook time: 30 minutes / Serves 4

Ingredients
- 1 kg rib-eye steaks (bone-in), cut into 4 pieces
- 1 tbsp olive oil
- Sea salt and ground black pepper, to taste
- 50g butter, softened, plus a little extra
- 1 red chilli, finely chopped
- 1 tbsp fresh lemon juice

Instructions
1. Pat the rib-eye steaks dry with kitchen towels. Place the steaks in two roasting trays and lower them into the cooking basket. Brush them with olive oil and season with salt and pepper to taste.
2. Select zone 1 and pair it with "AIR FRY" at 200°C for 30 minutes. Select "MATCH" to duplicate settings across both zones. Press the "START/STOP" button.
3. In the meantime, thoroughly combine the butter, chilli, and lemon juice. Chill until firm. When zone 1 time reaches 15 minutes, spread over the top of the steaks.
4. Reinsert the drawers to continue cooking.
5. Bon appétit!

Glazed Spare Ribs

Prep time: 5 minutes / Cook time: 40 minutes / Serves 4

Ingredients
- 1kg spare rib, cut between the bones
- 1 tsp ground allspice
- 1 tsp ground ginger
- 500ml ginger beer
- 2 limes, freshly squeezed
- 100ml tomato ketchup
- 20ml soy sauce
- 1 tbsp clear honey
- 1 tbsp vegetable oil

Instructions
1. Pat the rib-eye steaks dry with kitchen towels. Place the ribs in two roasting trays and lower them into the cooking basket.
2. Select zone 1 and pair it with "AIR FRY" at 180°C for 40 minutes. Select "MATCH" to duplicate settings across both zones. Press the "START/STOP" button.
3. Baste the ribs with the reserved marinade after every 10 minutes. Reinsert the drawers to continue cooking.
4. Bon appétit!

Festive Meatloaf

Prep time: 10 minutes / Cook time: 24 minutes / Serves 6

Ingredients

- 300g pork mince
- 400g beef mince
- 100g pancetta, cut into thin lardons
- 1 thick stale bread slice
- 1 large egg, beaten
- 1 small chilli pepper, deseeded and minced
- 1 medium leek, chopped
- 2 garlic cloves, minced
- 1 tsp red pepper flakes, crushed
- 100g rolled oats
- 1 tbsp butter
- 200ml tomato paste
- 1 tbsp Dijon mustard
- 1 tbsp clear honey

Instructions

1. Brush two loaf tins with nonstick cooking oil.
2. In a mixing bowl, thoroughly combine the meat, pancetta, bread slice, egg, chilli pepper, leek, garlic, parsley, oats, and butter.
3. Scrape the mixture into the prepared loaf tins. Spray the top of your meatloaves with cooking oil. Add a loaf tin to each drawer.
4. Mix the tomato paste, mustard, and honey for the glaze and set it aside.
5. Select zone 1 and pair it with "AIR FRY" at 180°C for 24 minutes. Select "MATCH" to duplicate settings across both zones. Press the "START/STOP" button.
6. When zone 1 time reaches 11 minutes, spread the glaze mixture over the top of your meatloaves and bake for a further 11 minutes, until the centre of your meatloaf reaches 74°C. Reinsert the drawer to continue cooking.
7. Let your meatloaves sit for 5 to 10 minutes before slicing and serving. Bon appétit!

Crackled Pork Belly with Cabbage

Prep time: 10 minutes / Cook time: 50 minutes / Serves 4

Ingredients

- 500g pork belly
- 2 tbsp hoisin sauce
- 1 tbsp clear honey
- 1 tbsp rice vinegar
- 1 tbsp soy sauce
- 500g red cabbage, cut into wedges
- 1 tsp olive oil
- Sea salt and ground black pepper, to taste

Instructions

1. Pat the pork belly dry with kitchen towels. In a small mixing bowl, whisk the hoisin sauce, honey, vinegar, and soy sauce; reserve.
2. Toss cabbage wedges with olive oil, salt, and black pepper to taste.
3. Now, place the pork belly in the zone 1 drawer and the cabbage in the zone 2 drawer; then, insert drawers in the unit.
4. Select zone 1 and pair it with "AIR FRY" at 160°C for 50 minutes. Select zone 2 and pair it with "AIR FRY" at 180°C for 10 minutes. Select "SYNC" followed by the "START/STOP" button.
5. When zone 1 time reaches 25 minutes, turn the pork belly over; reinsert the drawer to continue cooking.
6. When zone 2 time reaches 11 minutes, shake the drawer and reinsert it to continue cooking.

Mozzarella-Stuffed Pork Medallions

Prep time: 10 minutes / Cook time: 30 minutes / Serves 4-5

Ingredients

- 1 kg pork medallions
- A small bunch of sage, leaves picked
- 200g ball mozzarella, sliced into 16 pieces
- Sea salt and cayenne pepper, to taste
- 1 tbsp olive oil

Instructions

1. Cut the pork into 2 medallions.
2. Place the pork medallions on a board and make a deep pocket in the side with the tip of a sharp knife (do not cut all the way through).
3. Stuff each pocket with sage leaves and mozzarella. Thread a cocktail stick through the opening to close each pocket, season them with salt and pepper, and brush with olive oil.
4. Lower pork medallions into the drawers.
5. Select zone 1 and pair it with "ROAST" at 180°C for 30 minutes. Select "MATCH" to duplicate settings across both zones. Press the "START/STOP" button.
6. When zone 1 time reaches 15 minutes, turn the medallions over to ensure even browning. Reinsert the drawer to continue cooking.
7. Bon appétit!

Roast Beef with Parsnip

Prep time: 1 hour / Cook time: 45 minutes / Serves 4

Ingredients

- 500g beef top rump joint, sliced
- 50ml dry red wine
- 1 tbsp English mustard
- 2 tbsp soy sauce
- 1 garlic clove, minced

- 2 green onions, sliced
- Sea salt and ground black pepper, to taste
- 300g parsnip, sliced into 1cm chunks
- 2 tsp vegetable oil

Instructions

1. In a ceramic bowl, place the beef, wine, mustard, soy sauce, garlic, onion, salt, and black pepper. Allow it to marinate for at least 1 hour.
2. Toss the parsnips with salt, pepper, and 1 teaspoon of vegetable oil.
3. Place the beef slices in the zone 1 drawer and brush them with 1 teaspoon of vegetable oil. Reserve the marinade.
4. Place the parsnips in the zone 2 drawer.
5. Select zone 1 and pair it with "ROAST" at 195°C for 45 minutes. Select zone 2 and pair it with "ROAST" at 190°C for 15 minutes. Select "SYNC" followed by the "START/STOP" button.
6. At the halfway point, flip the beef slices over and baste them with the reserved marinade; reinsert the drawers to resume cooking.
7. Bon appétit!

Old-Fashioned Meatballs

Prep time: 10 minutes / Cook time: 20 minutes / Serves 6

Ingredients

- 600g beef mince
- 200g pork mince
- 1 medium egg, beaten
- 1 medium leek, chopped
- 2 garlic cloves, minced
- 100g rolled oats
- Sea salt and ground black pepper, to taste
- 2 tsp vegetable oil

Instructions

1. Insert a crisper plate in each drawer. Spray the crisper plates with nonstick cooking oil.
2. Thoroughly combine all the Ingredients until everything is well incorporated. Shape the meat mixture into balls and brush them with vegetable oil.
3. Arrange the meatballs in the cooking basket.
4. Select zone 1 and pair it with "AIR FRY" at 190°C for 20 minutes. Select "MATCH" to duplicate settings across both zones. Press the "START/STOP" button.
5. When zone 1 time reaches 10 minutes, shake the basket and reinsert the drawers to resume cooking.
6. Bon appétit!

Roast Lamb Chops with Winter Squash

Prep time: 10 minutes / Cook time: 15 minutes / Serves 4

Ingredients

- 4 lamb loin chops (120g each), 2.5cm thick
- 1 tbsp steak seasoning mix
- 400g winter squash, cut into 1.5cm pieces
- 1 tsp sesame oil
- 1 tbsp fresh mint leaves, finely chopped
- Sea salt and ground black pepper, to taste

Instructions

1. Toss lamb loin chops with steak seasoning mix and place them in the zone 1 drawer. Spray them with cooking oil.
2. Toss winter squash with sesame oil, salt, and pepper, and place them in the zone 2 drawer.
3. Select zone 1 and pair it with "AIR FRY" at 200°C for 15 minutes. Select "MATCH" to duplicate settings across both zones. Press the "START/STOP" button.
4. At the halfway point, shake your food or toss it with silicone-tipped tongs to promote even cooking. Enjoy!

Pork Chops with Mustardy Green Beans

Prep time: 20 minutes / Cook time: 20 minutes / Serves 4

Ingredients

- 4 pork chops (120g each)
- Sea salt and ground black pepper, to taste
- 1 tsp red pepper flakes, crushed
- 1 small garlic clove, crushed
- 400g fresh green beans, drained and rinsed
- 1 tsp sesame oil
- 50ml double cream
- 1 tsp wholegrain mustard

Instructions

1. Toss pork chops with salt, black pepper, and red pepper flakes, and place them in the zone 1 drawer. Spray them with cooking oil.
2. Toss green beans with sesame oil, salt, black pepper, double cream, and mustard. Now, arrange them in the zone 2 drawer.
3. Select zone 1 and pair it with "AIR FRY" at 200°C for 20 minutes. Select zone 2 and pair it with "ROAST" at 190°C for 12 minutes. Select "SYNC" followed by the "START/STOP" button.
4. At the halfway point, flip or toss your food to promote even browning; reinsert the drawers to resume cooking.
5. Bon appétit!

CHAPTER 7 SNACKS & APPETIZERS

Roast Squash with Goat's Cheese

Prep time: 10 minutes / Cook time: 20 minutes / Serves 4

Ingredients

- 1kg delicata (or butternut) squash, cubed
- 1 tbsp butter, melted
- 1 tsp cayenne pepper
- Sea salt and ground black pepper, to taste
- 10 sage leaves
- 100g soft goat's cheese

Instructions

1. Insert crisper plates in both drawers. Spray the crisper plates with nonstick cooking oil.
2. Brush the squash with butter, cayenne pepper, salt, and black pepper. Place the squash pieces in both drawers.
3. Select zone 1 and pair it with "ROAST" at 200°C for 20 minutes. Select "MATCH" followed by the "START/STOP" button.
4. Turn over the squash pieces halfway through the cooking time. Top them with cheese and reinsert the drawers to resume cooking.
5. Garnish roasted squash with sage leaves.
6. Bon appétit!

Beet & Chorizo Salad

Prep time: 10 minutes / Cook time: 40 minutes / Serves 4-5

Ingredients

- 300g chorizo, skinned and thickly sliced
- 500g red beets, peeled, whole
- 1 tbsp extra-virgin olive oil
- 1 tbsp sherry vinegar
- 1 tsp stone-ground mustard
- 1/2 tsp cumin, ground
- Sea salt and ground black pepper, to taste
- 1 small bulb of garlic
- 1/2 small bunch parsley, roughly chopped
- 50g manchego, shaved

Instructions

1. Insert crisper plates in both drawers. Spray the crisper plates with nonstick cooking oil. Place the beets in the zone 1 drawer and the chorizo in the zone 2 drawer.
2. Select zone 1 and pair it with "AIR FRY" at 200°C for 40 minutes. Select zone 2 and pair it with "AIR FRY" at 190°C for 15 minutes. Select "SYNC" followed by the "START/STOP" button.
3. At the halfway point, turn the beets over to ensure even cooking; wrap the garlic bulb in foil and place it in the zone 1 drawer. Now, reinsert the drawers to resume cooking.
4. Now, squeeze the roasted garlic cloves out of their skins; mash them with a fork.
5. Let the beets cool and remove the skin. Cut your beets into slices and toss them with the remaining Ingredients.
6. To serve, top your salad with the sliced chorizo and enjoy!

Sticky Wings

Prep time: 1 hour / Cook time: 33 minutes / Serves 4

Ingredients

- 1kg chicken wings, drumettes & flats
- 2 tbsp Worcestershire sauce
- 1 tsp English mustard powder
- 1/2 tsp garlic granules
- 1/2 tsp onion powder
- 1/2 tsp ground cumin
- 1 tbsp butter, melted
- 2 tbsp clear honey
- Sea salt and ground black pepper, to taste

Instructions

1. Place all the Ingredients in a ceramic (or glass) bowl. Cover the bowl and let the chicken wings marinate for approximately 1 hour in the fridge.
2. Drain and reserve the marinade.
3. Insert crisper plates in both drawers. Spray the crisper plates with nonstick cooking oil. Divide the wings between drawers.
4. Select zone 1 and pair it with "AIR FRY" at 200°C for 33 minutes. Select "MATCH" followed by the "START/STOP" button.
5. At the halfway point, turn the wings over, baste them with the reserved marinade, and reinsert the drawers to resume cooking. Devour!

Garlicky Okra Chips

Prep time: 10 minutes / Cook time: 20 minutes / Serves 5

Ingredients

- 1kg okra, cut into halves lengthwise
- 2 garlic cloves, crushed
- 1 tsp ground coriander
- 1 tsp turmeric powder
- Sea salt and ground black pepper, to taste
- 2 tbsp soy sauce
- 1 tbsp butter
- 50g breadcrumbs
- 50g Parmesan cheese, preferably freshly grated

Instructions

1. Toss okra halves with garlic, spices, soy sauce, and butter until they are well coated on all sides.
2. Add okra to both drawers of your Ninja Foodi (with a crisper plate inserted).
3. Select zone 1 and pair it with "AIR FRY" at 180°C for 20 minutes. Select "MATCH" followed by the "START/STOP" button.
4. At the halfway point, shake the drawers and top the okra with breadcrumbs and cheese; reinsert the drawers to resume cooking.
5. Serve okra chips with a dipping sauce on the side and enjoy!

Kid-Friendly Mozzarella Sticks

Prep time: 10 minutes / Cook time: 8 minutes / Serves 6

Ingredients

- 500g block firm mozzarella cheese, cut into 1cm-thick finger-length strips
- 120g all-purpose flour
- 1 large egg
- 150g crushed tortilla chips
- 1 tsp dried oregano
- 1 tsp dried basil
- 1 tsp garlic granules
- 1 tsp dried parsley flakes
- Sea salt and ground black pepper, to taste
- 1 tbsp olive oil

Instructions

1. Insert crisper plates in both drawers. Spray the crisper plates with nonstick cooking oil.
2. Set up your breading station. Tip the flour into a shallow bowl. In a separate bowl, whisk the egg. Lastly, thoroughly combine crushed tortilla chips with spices in a third dish.
3. Start by dredging mozzarella sticks in the flour; then, dip them into the egg. Press mozzarella sticks into

the seasoned crumbs.
4. Brush breaded mozzarella sticks with olive oil and arrange them in both drawers.
5. Select zone 1 and pair it with "AIR FRY" at 190°C for 8 minutes. Select "MATCH" followed by the "START/STOP" button.
6. At the halfway point, turn the mozzarella sticks over to ensure even cooking; reinsert the drawers to resume cooking.
7. Taste and adjust the seasoning. Bon appétit!

Crisp Chicken Bites

Prep time: 10 minutes / Cook time: 15 minutes / Serves 6

Ingredients

- 800g chicken breast fillets, cut into bite-sized pieces
- 2 tbsp pesto sauce
- 2 tbsp mayonnaise
- 150g tortilla chips, crushed
- 2 tsp olive oil

Instructions

1. Coat chicken pieces with the pesto and mayonnaise.
2. Then, roll each piece of the chicken onto crushed tortilla chips, pressing to adhere.
3. Brush the chicken pieces with olive oil and lower them into the cooking basket.
4. Select zone 1 and pair it with "AIR FRY" at 200°C for 15 minutes. Select "MATCH" followed by the "START/STOP" button.
5. Serve with your favourite sauce for dipping and enjoy!

Twisted Halloumi Pigs in Blankets

Prep time: 10 minutes / Cook time: 15 minutes / Serves 6

Ingredients

- 5 rashers pancetta, cut into halves lengthwise
- 10 (20g each) halloumi pieces, casing removed
- 1 tsp English mustard powder
- 1 tsp hot paprika

Instructions

1. Insert crisper plates in both drawers. Spray the crisper plates with nonstick cooking oil.
2. Wrap halloumi pieces in the pancetta slices and arrange them in both drawers if your Ninja Foodi. Sprinkle them with mustard powder and paprika.
3. Select zone 1 and pair it with "AIR FRY" at 180°C for 15 minutes. Select "MATCH" followed by the

"START/STOP" button.

4. At the halfway point, turn the pigs-in-blankets over, and reinsert the drawers to resume cooking. Enjoy!

Parmesan Brussels Sprouts

Prep time: 5 minutes / Cook time: 20 minutes / Serves 4

Ingredients

- 1 kg Brussels sprouts, halved, stem removed
- Sea salt and ground black pepper, to taste
- 1/2 tsp fennel seeds, ground
- 1 tbsp cayenne pepper
- 1 tsp garlic granules
- 1 tbsp olive oil
- 200g Parmesan cheese, grated

Instructions

1. Toss Brussels sprouts with spices and olive oil until well-coated on all sides. Arrange Brussels sprouts in the lightly-greased drawers.
2. Select zone 1 and pair it with "AIR FRY" at 190°C for 20 minutes. Select "MATCH" to duplicate settings across both zones. Press the "START/STOP" button.
3. When zone 1 time reaches 10 minutes, top Brussels sprouts with Parmesan cheese; reinsert drawers to continue cooking.
4. Bon appétit!

Moroccan-Style Meatball Bites

Prep time: 10 minutes / Cook time: 20 minutes / Serves 9

Ingredients

- 300g turkey mince
- 300g beef mince
- 100g bacon lardons
- 20g ground almonds
- 1 medium egg, beaten
- 1 medium onion, chopped
- 2 garlic cloves, minced
- 100g rolled oats
- Sea salt and ground black pepper, to taste
- 2 tsp vegetable oil

Instructions

1. Insert a crisper plate in each drawer. Spray the crisper plates with nonstick cooking oil.
2. Thoroughly combine all the Ingredients until everything is well incorporated. Shape the meat mixture into balls and brush them with vegetable oil.
3. Arrange the meatballs on the prepared drawers.

4. Select zone 1 and pair it with "AIR FRY" at 190°C for 20 minutes. Select "MATCH" to duplicate settings across both zones. Press the "START/STOP" button.
5. When zone 1 time reaches 10 minutes, shake the basket and reinsert the drawers to resume cooking.
6. Serve meatballs with cocktail sticks and enjoy!

Herbed Roast Potatoes

Prep time: 10 minutes / Cook time: 20 minutes / Serves 6-8

Ingredients

- 800g Charlotte or Nicola potatoes, quartered
- 1 tsp olive oil
- Sea salt and ground black pepper, to taste
- 1 tsp butter, melted
- 1 tsp dried parsley flakes
- 1 tbsp dried basil
- 1 tsp dried rosemary

Instructions

1. Toss your potatoes with olive oil, salt, and black pepper.
2. Select zone 1 and pair it with "AIR FRY" at 190°C for 20 minutes. Select "MATCH" to duplicate settings across both zones. Press the "START/STOP" button.
3. When zone 1 time reaches 10 minutes, shake the basket and toss your potatoes with butter and herbs. Reinsert the drawers to resume cooking.
4. Serve with cocktail sticks and enjoy!

Glazed Lemon Baby Carrots

Prep time: 10 minutes / Cook time: 15 minutes / Serves 5-6

Ingredients

- 800g baby carrots, whole
- 1 tbsp sesame (or avocado oil) oil
- Sea salt and ground black pepper, to taste
- 1 tsp dried parsley flakes
- 1/2 tsp dried dill
- 1 tbsp clear honey
- Zest and juice of 1 lemon

Instructions

1. Toss baby carrots with sesame oil, salt, and black pepper.
2. Select zone 1 and pair it with "AIR FRY" at 180°C for 15 minutes. Select "MATCH" to duplicate settings across both zones. Press the "START/STOP" button.
3. When zone 1 time reaches 8 minutes, shake the basket and toss your carrots. Reinsert the drawers to resume cooking.
4. In the meantime, mix the remaining Ingredients until

everything is well combined.

5. Drizzle over the dressing, and, then transfer to a serving bowl. Devour!

Roasted Cabbage and Cherry Tomatoes

Prep time: 10 minutes / Cook time: 10 minutes / Serves 6

Ingredients

- 400g cabbage, cut into wedges
- 500g cherry tomatoes
- 2 tsp olive oil
- Sea salt and ground black pepper, to taste
- 1 tsp cayenne pepper
- 1 tbsp dried oregano
- 1 tbsp dried basil
- 50g goat cheese, crumbled

Instructions

1. Toss your cabbage and cherry tomatoes with olive oil, salt, black pepper, cayenne pepper, oregano, and basil.
2. Place the cabbage in the zone 1 drawer and cherry tomatoes in the zone 2 drawer; then, insert drawers in the unit.
3. Select zone 1 and pair it with "AIR FRY" at 170°C for 10 minutes. Select zone 2 and pair it with "AIR FRY" at 200°C for 5 minutes. Select "SYNC" followed by the "START/STOP" button.
4. At the halfway point, turn your food over to ensure even cooking; top with cheese. Now, reinsert the drawers to resume cooking.
5. Garnish your vegetables with fresh herbs and enjoy!

Courgette Chips

Prep time: 5 minutes / Cook time: 12 minutes / Serves 5-6

Ingredients

- 1 pound courgette, cut into 1cm stick
- 1 tsp olive oil
- 1/2 tsp garlic granules
- 1/2 tsp. cayenne pepper
- 1/2 tsp garlic granules
- Sea salt and ground black pepper, to taste
- 200g Parmesan cheese, preferably freshly grated

Instructions

1. Insert a crisper plate in each drawer. Spray the crisper plates with nonstick cooking oil.
2. Toss your courgette with olive oil and spices.
3. Select zone 1 and pair it with "AIR FRY" at 200°C for 12 minutes. Select "MATCH" to duplicate settings

across both zones. Press the "START/STOP" button.
4. When zone 1 time reaches 6 minutes, shake the basket and top the sticks with Parmesan cheese. Reinsert the drawers to resume cooking.
5. Bon appétit!

Corn on the Cob with Chilli Butter

Prep time: 5 minutes / Cook time: 10 minutes / Serves 4

Ingredients

- 4 corn cobs, halved
- 40g butter, softened
- 1 garlic clove, crushed
- 2 tsp fresh chilli, chopped
- 1 tbsp fresh cilantro leaves, minced

Instructions

1. In a small mixing bowl, thoroughly combine the butter, garlic, and chilli. Cut 8 pieces of tin foil and place 1/2 of the cob on each piece. Now, top them with the chili butter and seal the edges to form the packets.
2. Transfer the packets to the cooking basket.
3. Select zone 1 and pair it with "AIR FRY" at 170°C for 10 minutes. Select "MATCH" to duplicate settings across both zones. Press the "START/STOP" button.
4. When zone 1 time reaches 6 minutes, shake the basket and top the sticks with Parmesan cheese. Reinsert the drawers to resume cooking.
5. Enjoy!

Cabbage with Garlic-Thyme Butter

Prep time: 5 minutes / Cook time: 15 minutes / Serves 4

Ingredients

- 1 green cabbage head, cleaned and cut into wedges
- 1 tsp olive oil
- Sea salt and ground black pepper, to taste
- 2 tbsp butter, melted
- 1 garlic clove, minced
- 1 tsp dried thyme
- 1 tbsp lemon zest, grated

Instructions

1. Toss the cabbage wedges with the olive oil, salt, ad black pepper and transfer them to the lightly-greased cooking basket.
2. Select zone 1 and pair it with "ROAST" at 180°C for 15 minutes. Select "MATCH" to duplicate settings across both zones. Press the "START/STOP" button.
3. Meanwhile, mix the other Ingredients until well

combined; set it aside.

4. When zone 1 time reaches 7 minutes, turn the cabbage wedges over and top them with the butter mixture. Reinsert the drawers to resume cooking.

5. Cook until crisp-tender and enjoy!

Sweet Potato Crisps

Prep time: 20 minutes / Cook time: 20 minutes / Serves 4-6

Ingredients
- 800g sweet potatoes, peeled and cut into 1/2-cm thick slices
- 1 tbsp olive oil
- 1 tsp dried cumin
- Coarse sea salt and ground black pepper, to taste
- 1 tbsp Italian seasoning mix
- 100 gm blue cheese, crumbled
- for serving, optional

Instructions
1. Place sweet potato slices in a bowl of cold water; let sweet potatoes sit for about 20 minutes.
2. Toss sweet potato slices with the olive oil and spices. Add sweet potato slices to both drawers.
3. Select zone 1 and pair it with "AIR FRY" at 190°C for 20 minutes. Select "MATCH" to duplicate settings across both zones. Press the "START/STOP" button.
4. When zone 1 time reaches 10 minutes, toss your crisps and top them with cheese. Reinsert the drawers to resume cooking.
5. Serve sweet potato crisps with a light ranch dressing, if desired. Bon appétit!

Cheesy Butternut Squash Mash

Prep time: 20 minutes / Cook time: 25 minutes / Serves 5

Ingredients
- 800g butternut squash, peeled and cut into 1cm chunks
- 1 tsp sesame oil (or peanut oil)
- 1 tsp garlic granules
- 1/2 tsp ground anise
- 100g sharp cheese, grated
- 1 tbsp fresh cilantro leaves, roughly chopped

Instructions
1. Toss butternut squash chunks with sesame (or peanut) oil and spices. Lower the butternut squash chunks into both drawers.
2. Select zone 1 and pair it with "AIR FRY" at 195°C for 15 minutes. Select "MATCH" to duplicate settings across both zones. Press the "START/STOP" button.
3. When zone 1 time reaches 7 minutes, shake the

basket and reinsert the drawers to resume cooking.

4. Purée the butternut squash using an immersion blender or potato masher. Transfer the butternut squash mash to a casserole dish and top it with cheese.
5. Select zone 1 and pair it with "ROAST" at 155°C for 10 minutes. Press the "START/STOP" button.
6. Garnish butternut squash mash with fresh cilantro leaves.
7. Bon appétit!

Garlicky Green Beans

Prep time: 10 minutes / Cook time: 20 minutes / Serves 4-5

Ingredients
- 400g fresh green beans, drained and rinsed
- 1 tsp vegetable oil
- Sea salt and ground black pepper, to taste
- 1 small bulb of garlic
- 1 tbsp butter, room temperature

Instructions
1. Toss green beans with vegetable oil, salt, and black pepper. Arrange them in the zone 1 drawer.
2. Wrap the garlic bulb in foil and place it in the zone 2 drawer.
3. Select zone 1 and pair it with "ROAST" at 200°C for 5 minutes. Select zone 2 and pair it with "ROAST" at 200°C for 20 minutes. Select "SYNC" followed by the "START/STOP" button.
4. Next, squeeze the roasted garlic cloves out of their skins and mash them with butter. Top roasted green beans with garlic butter and enjoy!

Crispy Mushroom Bites

Prep time: 10 minutes / Cook time: 12 minutes / Serves 6

Ingredients
- 600g button mushrooms, cleaned and stems removed
- 2 large eggs
- 1/2 tsp onion powder
- 1 tsp garlic granules
- 1 tsp dried parsley flakes
- Sea salt and ground black pepper, to taste
- 100g plain flour
- 150g dried breadcrumbs
- 1 tbsp olive oil

Instructions
1. Insert crisper plates in both drawers. Spray crisper plates with nonstick cooking oil. Pat the mushrooms dry using paper towels.
2. Now, make the breading station: Beat the eggs until pale and frothy. In a separate shallow dish, mix the

spices and flour. In a third shallow dish, thoroughly combine the breadcrumbs with olive oil.

3. Dip the mushrooms in the egg, then, dust your mushrooms with the flour mixture. Roll them over the breadcrumb mixture, pressing to adhere.
4. Arrange the prepared mushrooms on the crisper plates.
5. Select zone 1 and pair it with "AIR FRY" at 190°C for 12 minutes. Select "MATCH" to duplicate settings across both zones. Press the "START/STOP" button.
6. When zone 1 time reaches 6 minutes, turn the mushrooms over using silicone-tipped tongs. Reinsert the drawers to continue cooking.
7. Serve the mushrooms with a dipping sauce of choice. Enjoy!

Pancetta Wrapped Lemon Scallops

Prep time: 5 minutes / Cook time: 8 minutes / Serves 7-8

Ingredients
- 15 scallops
- 1 tbsp lemon juice, freshly squeezed
- Sea salt and ground black pepper, to taste
- 1 tsp red pepper flakes, crushed
- 1 tsp honey
- 15 thin rashers streaky bacon

Instructions
1. Insert crisper plates in both drawers. Spray crisper plates with nonstick cooking oil.
2. Toss your scallops with lemon juice, salt, black pepper, red pepper, and honey.
3. Wrap one rasher of bacon around each scallop; secure with toothpicks. Arrange the pancetta-wrapped scallops on the crisper plates in both drawers.
4. Select zone 1 and pair it with "AIR FRY" at 200°C for 7 to 8 minutes. Select "MATCH" to duplicate settings across both zones. Press the "START/STOP" button.
5. When zone 1 time reaches 4 minutes, turn the scallops over using silicone-tipped tongs. Reinsert the drawers to continue cooking. Enjoy!

Crispy Karachi Chickpeas

Prep time: 5 minutes / Cook time: 15minutes / Serves 4

Ingredients
- 550g chickpeas, drained
- 1 tbsp olive oil
- ¾ tbsp mixed masala
- ½ tsp onion powder
- ½ tsp garlic powder
- 30ml lemon juice

Instructions

1. Preheat the dual zone to 200°C for 5 minutes
2. Meanwhile, toss all of the Ingredients into a mixing bowl (except lemon juice) and carefully combine with a wooden spoon
3. Divide the chickpeas between both zone draws
4. Pair the zone draws to 'ROAST' at 200°C for 13 minutes
5. Press 'MATCH' followed by 'START/STOP' to begin cooking the chickpeas
6. At the halfway point of cooking, drizzle some lemon juice over the chickpeas and give them a shake
7. At the end of the cooking time, remove the chickpeas and divide them between 4 small bowls, then serve

Popcorn Kidney Beans

Prep time: 5 minutes / Cook time: 25 minutes / Serves 4

Ingredients
- 550g Red kidney beans
- 1 cal olive oil fry spray
- 1 ¼ tsp sea salt

Instructions
1. Preheat the dual zone to 180°C for 5 minutes with the crisper plate
2. Meanwhile, toss the kidney beans in a mixing bowl, spray them then dash salt on top
3. Divide the kidney beans between both zone draws
4. Pair the zone draws to 'AIR FRY' at 180°C for 25 minutes
5. Press 'MATCH' followed by 'START/STOP' to begin cooking the kidney beans
6. At the halfway point of cooking, give the kidney beans a shake
7. Retrieve the kidney beans once they have split, then serve

Garlic Green Beans

Prep time: 5 minutes / Cook time: 10 minutes / Serves 4

Ingredients
- 100g green beans
- 1/4 teaspoon of garlic powder
- 1/4 teaspoons of salt
- 1/4 teaspoon of black pepper
- 2 tablespoons of olive oil
- 50g bacon lardons (optional)

Instructions
1. Wash your green beans and remove the ends.
2. Coat your green beans in the oil.
3. Toss the oiled beans in the seasoning.
4. Place the green beans into your air fryer tray.
5. Add your bacon lardons if choosing to.
6. Air fry at 180 degrees Celsius for 8-10 minutes, shaking halfway through.

CHAPTER 8 HEALTHY VEGETARIAN & VEGAN RECIPES

Vegetarian Cottage Pie

Prep time: 10 minutes / Cook time: 43 minutes / Serves 6

Ingredients

- 1 tbsp olive oil
- 1 large bell pepper, sliced
- 1 large carrot, chopped
- 1 large onion, chopped
- 1 large parsnip, chopped
- 500g chestnut mushrooms, sliced
- 4 tbsp tomato purée
- 200ml vegetable broth
- 1kg potatoes, cut into chunks
- 50g butter
- 4 tbsp whole milk

Instructions

1. Heat the oil in a medium saucepan over medium-high flame; sauté bell pepper, carrot, onion, and parsnip for about 3 minutes, until they've softened; reserve.
2. In the same pan, cook the mushrooms for about 3 minutes, until no longer pink. Add the tomato purée.
3. Pour over the broth, add the vegetables back to the pan, and spoon the mixture into an ovenproof dish.
4. Add potatoes to the zone 1 drawer; add the ovenproof dish to the zone 2 drawer.
5. Select zone 1 and pair it with "ROAST" at 190°C for 22 minutes. Select zone 2 and pair it with "AIR FRY" at 180°C for 20 minutes.
6. Select "SYNC" followed by the "START/STOP" button. At the halfway point, shake the drawer with potatoes to promote even cooking.
7. Mash the potatoes with butter and milk. Top your pie with the mash and ruffle with a fork.
8. Bake at 180°C for 15 minutes until the top is starting to colour. Enjoy!

Vegetable and Egg Cups

Prep time: 10 minutes / Cook time: 15 minutes / Serves 8

Ingredients

- 8 eggs
- 2 tbsp cream cheese
- 100g double cream
- 2 spring onions, thinly sliced
- 1 large garlic clove, minced
- 2 bell peppers, seeded and chopped
- 1 medium tomato, chopped
- 200g baby spinach, torn into pieces
- 1 tsp red pepper flakes, crushed
- Sea salt and ground black pepper, to taste

Instructions

1. Spray 8 muffin cases with cooking oil. Remove the crisper plates from your Ninja Dual Zone Air Fryer.
2. In a mixing bowl, thoroughly combine all the Ingredients. Spoon the batter into the prepared muffin cases.
3. Place mini frittatas in both drawers.
4. Select zone 1 and pair it with "BAKE" at 180°C for 15 minutes. Select "MATCH" followed by the "START/STOP" button.
5. Bon appétit!

Smoky Aubergine Burger

Prep time: 10 minutes / Cook time: 15 minutes / Serves 6

Ingredients

- 1 medium aubergine, wide middle section cut into 6 rounds
- 1 tbsp olive oil
- 1 tsp smoked paprika
- 1/2 tsp ground cumin
- 1/2 tsp English mustard powder
- Sea salt and ground black pepper, to taste
- 2 tbsp cornmeal
- 6 ciabatta rolls, halved
- 6 tbsp tofu mayonnaise
- 1 medium tomato, sliced

- 1 medium onion, sliced into rings

Instructions

1. Insert crisper plates in both drawers. Spray crisper plates with nonstick cooking oil.
2. Toss the aubergine rounds with olive oil, spices, and cornmeal. Toss until they are well coated on all sides.
3. Arrange aubergine rounds on the prepared crisper plates.
4. Select zone 1 and pair it with "BAKE" at 190°C for 15 minutes. Select "MATCH" followed by the "START/STOP" button.
5. Spread the rolls with tofu mayonnaise. Place aubergine rounds, tomatoes, and onion slices on top. Enjoy!

Classic Cauliflower Wings

Prep time: 5 minutes / Cook time: 13 minutes / Serves 4

Ingredients

- 1kg cauliflower florets
- 1 tbsp olive oil
- 1 tbsp soy sauce
- 1/2 tsp hot paprika
- 1/2 tsp onion granules
- 1/2 tsp garlic granules
- Sea salt and ground black pepper, to taste

Instructions

1. Place the cauliflower florets, along with the other Ingredients, in a resealable bag; give it a good shake until the cauliflower florets are well coated on all sides.
2. Arrange cauliflower florets on two roasting tins. Lower the roasting tins into the cooking basket.
3. Select zone 1 and pair it with "ROAST" at 200°C for 13 minutes. Select "MATCH" followed by the "START/STOP" button.
4. When zone 1 time reaches 7 minutes, shake the basket and reinsert the drawers to resume cooking. Cook until crisp-tender and enjoy!
5. Bon appétit!

Chips with Mushy Peas

Prep time: 5 minutes / Cook time: 20 minutes / Serves 4

Ingredients

- 500g baking potatoes, peeled and cut into thick chips

- 1 tbsp olive oil
- Sea salt and ground black pepper, to taste
- 200g frozen pea
- 1 tbsp butter
- 20g crème fraîche

Instructions

1. Toss your potatoes with olive oil, salt, and pepper. Now, boil the peas for approximately 4 minutes; drain and mash with butter, crème fraiche and salt to taste. Spoon the mixture into a lightly greased baking dish.
2. Place the potatoes in the zone 1 drawer and the baking tin in the zone 2 drawer.
3. Select zone 1 and pair it with "AIR FRY" at 190°C for 20 minutes. Select zone 2 and pair it with "BAKE" at 190°C for 10 minutes. Select "SYNC" followed by the "START/STOP" button.
4. At the halfway point, shake the basket with chips to promote even cooking; reinsert the drawer to resume cooking.
5. Bon appétit!

Harissa Cauliflower Pilaf

Prep time: 10 minutes / Cook time: 23 minutes / Serves 5

Ingredients

- 1 large cauliflower head, broken into small florets
- 300g can chickpeas, drained and rinsed
- 1 tbsp olive oil
- 250g basmati rice
- 1 medium onion, finely sliced
- 2 tbsp harissa
- 1 garlic clove, crushed
- 2 bay leaves
- 300ml hot vegan stock
- 1 tbsp fresh dill, chopped
- Sea salt and ground black pepper, to taste

Instructions

1. Toss cauliflower florets and chickpeas with olive oil.
2. Place the cauliflower florets in the zone 1 drawer and the chickpeas in the zone 2 drawer.
3. Select zone 1 and pair it with "AIR FRY" at 180°C for 10 minutes. Select zone 2 and pair it with "ROAST" at 200°C for 13 minutes. Select "SYNC" followed by the "START/STOP" button.
4. At the halfway point, toss your food to promote even cooking; reinsert the drawer to resume cooking.
5. Meanwhile, cook basmati rice according to the

manufacturer's Instructions. Drain the rice and tip into two roasting tins.

6. Pour over the vegan stock and mix well. Stir in the remaining Ingredients, including air-fried cauliflower and chickpeas.

7. Select zone 1 and pair it with "ROAST" at 180°C for 10 minutes. Select "MATCH" followed by the "START/STOP" button.

8. Bon appétit!

Vegan Quinoa Burgers

Prep time: 10 minutes / Cook time: 18 minutes / Serves 4

Ingredients

- 300g quinoa, soaked overnight and rinsed
- 300g canned white beans, drained and rinsed
- 1 medium onion, finely chopped
- 2 garlic cloves, crushed
- 2 tbsp vegan BBQ sauce
- 1 tbsp tahini
- Sea salt and ground black pepper, to taste
- 50 g breadcrumbs

Instructions

1. In a mixing bowl, thoroughly combine all the Ingredients. Shape the mixture into patties and arrange them in the lightly-greased Air Fryer cooking basket.

2. Select zone 1 and pair it with "AIR FRY" at 200°C for 18 minutes. Select "MATCH" followed by the "START/STOP" button.

3. Serve your burgers on buns and toppings of choice.

4. Bon appétit!

Tofu Sandwich with Roasted Peppers

Prep time: 10 minutes / Cook time: 15 minutes / Serves 4

Ingredients

- 400g block tofu
- 2 large bell peppers, deseeded and sliced
- 1 tsp olive oil
- Ground black pepper and cayenne pepper, to taste
- 1/2 tsp garlic granules
- 50g mayonnaise
- 1 large handful rocket
- 1 large ripe tomato, sliced
- 6 thick slices of focaccia or 8 slices of bread

Instructions

1. Press your tofu: Place the folded paper towels on a board. Place the block of tofu on the paper towels. Top the tofu with another layer of paper towels. Press it with a heavy pan or pot that is filled with water. Allow your tofu to stand for at least 30 minutes.

2. Cut your tofu into 6-8 slices and reserve. Toss bell peppers with olive oil, black pepper, cayenne pepper, and garlic granules.

3. Place the tofu slices in the zone 1 drawer and the peppers in the zone 2 drawer.

4. Select zone 1 and pair it with "AIR FRY" at 190°C for 14 minutes. Select zone 2 and pair it with "ROAST" at 200°C for 15 minutes. Select "SYNC" followed by the "START/STOP" button.

5. At the halfway point, toss your food to promote even cooking; reinsert the drawer to resume cooking.

6. Assemble 4 sandwiches with bread slices, mayonnaise, tofu, roasted pepper, rocket, and tomatoes. Serve and enjoy!

Halloumi Cheese Fingers

Prep time: 10 minutes / Cook time: 6 minutes / Serves 4

Ingredients

- 500g halloumi
- 100g plain flour
- 1 large egg
- 100g cornflakes, crushed
- 1 tbsp Greek seasoning mix
- 1 tsp vegetable oil

Instructions

1. Insert crisper plates in both drawers. Spray crisper plates with nonstick cooking oil. Cut the halloumi into fat chips.

2. Now, set up your breading station: Tip the flour into a shallow dish. In a separate dish, beat the egg until frothy. Lastly, combine the crushed cornflakes with Greek seasoning mix in a third dish.

3. Start by dredging halloumi pieces in the flour; then, dip them into the egg. Press halloumi into the cornflake mixture. Brush breaded halloumi pieces with olive oil and lower them onto crisper plates.

4. Select zone 1 and pair it with "AIR FRY" at 190°C for 6 minutes. Select "MATCH" followed by the "START/STOP" button.

5. Serve warm halloumi cheese fingers with a dipping sauce of choice.

6. Bon appétit!

Healthy Crispy Falafel

Prep time: 10 minutes / Cook time: 25 minutes / Serves 4

Ingredients

- 200g dried chickpeas, soaked overnight
- 40g breadcrumbs
- 1/2 tsp bicarbonate of soda
- 1 small leek, chopped
- 2 garlic cloves, minced
- 1 small bunch of parsley
- 1 tbsp tahini
- Sea salt and freshly ground black pepper, to taste
- 1 tbsp olive oil
- 4 pitta bread, to serve

Instructions

1. Insert crisper plates in both drawers. Spray crisper plates with nonstick cooking oil.
2. Add all Ingredients, except pita bread, to a bowl of your food processor or a high-speed blender. Blend until everything is well combined.
3. Shape the mixture into equal balls using damp hands; arrange them on the prepared crisper plates.
4. Select zone 1 and pair it with "AIR FRY" at 190°C for 20 minutes. Select "MATCH" followed by the "START/STOP" button.
5. Toast pitta bread at 190°C for 5 minutes until they are lightly charred. Serve your falafel with toasted pita bread and toppings of choice. Enjoy!

Vegan Nuggets

Prep time: 10 minutes / Cook time: 15 minutes / Serves 4-5

Ingredients

- 500g tofu, pressed
- 100g plain flour
- 60ml rice (or soy) milk
- 1/2 tsp baking powder
- 1/2 tsp turmeric powder
- 100g old-fashioned rolled oats
- 1 tsp garlic granules
- 1/2 tsp onion powder
- 1/2 tsp English mustard powder
- 20g nutritional yeast
- 1 tbsp olive oil

Instructions

1. Insert crisper plates in both drawers. Spray crisper plates with nonstick cooking oil.
2. Pat your tofu dry with tea towels and cut it into bite-sized chunks.
3. To begin, set up your breading station. Mix the flour with milk, baking powder, and turmeric powder in a shallow dish. In a separate dish, mix the oats, garlic granules, onion powder, mustard, and nutritional yeast.
4. Dip tofu cubes in the flour mixture. Then, press them into the oat mixture, coating evenly. Brush the tofu chunks with olive oil.
5. Place the vegan nuggets on the prepared crisper plates. Select zone 1 and pair it with "AIR FRY" at 190°C for 15 minutes. Select "MATCH" followed by the "START/STOP" button.
6. At the halfway point, turn the vegan nuggets over and reinsert the drawer to resume cooking.
7. Bon appétit!

Chickpea Sausage with Sticky Brussels Sprouts

Prep time: 10 minutes / Cook time: 20 minutes / Serves 4-5

Ingredients

- Chickpea Sausage:
- 240g can chickpea, drained
- 2 tbsp sunflower seeds
- 2 tbsp walnut halves
- 1 medium onion, peeled and quartered
- 4 garlic cloves, peeled
- 60g chickpea flour
- 1/2 tsp bicarbonate of soda
- 1 tbsp tahini
- Sea salt and freshly ground black pepper, to taste
- 1 tbsp olive oil
- Sticky Brussels Sprouts:
- 400g Brussels sprouts, trimmed and halved
- 1 tsp olive oil
- 1 tbsp soy sauce
- 1 tbsp agave syrup
- 1 tbsp balsamic vinegar
- 1 tsp garlic granules
- Sea salt and ground black pepper, to taste

Instructions

1. In your blender or food processor, blend all the Ingredients for the chickpea sausages. Blend until everything is well incorporated.
2. Shape the mixture into sausages and place them in the zone 1 drawer.
3. Toss Brussels sprouts with olive oil, soy sauce, agave syrup, vinegar, garlic granules, salt, and black

pepper until they are well coated on all sides. Add Brussels sprouts to the zone 2 drawer.

4. Select zone 1 and pair it with "AIR FRY" at 180°C for 20 minutes. Select zone 2 and pair it with "ROAST" at 190°C for 15 minutes. Select "SYNC" followed by the "START/STOP" button.

5. At the halfway point, toss your food to promote even cooking; reinsert the drawer to resume cooking.

6. Bon appétit!

Vegan Wraps

Prep time: 10 minutes / Cook time: 20 minutes / Serves 4

Ingredients
- 300g tempeh
- 300g carrots, cut into sticks
- 2 tbsp soy sauce (or coconut aminos)
- 1 tbsp rice vinegar
- 1 garlic clove, crushed
- 1 tbsp cornstarch
- 1/2 tsp ginger powder
- Sea salt and black pepper, to taste
- 1/2 tsp red pepper flakes, crushed
- 4 large tortillas
- 4 tbsp hummus
- 1 small avocado, peeled, pitted, and spiced
- 1 Little Gem lettuce, leaves separated
- 1 small tomato, sliced

Instructions
1. Toss tempeh and carrots with soy sauce, vinegar, garlic, cornstarch, and spices.
2. Add tempeh to the zone 1 drawer and carrots to the zone 2 drawer.
3. Select zone 1 and pair it with "AIR FRY" at 180°C for 8 minutes. Select zone 2 and pair it with "ROAST" at 190°C for 15 minutes. Select "SYNC" followed by the "START/STOP" button.
4. At the halfway point, toss your food to promote even cooking; reinsert the drawer to resume cooking.
5. Toast tortillas at 180°C for 5 minutes. Divide all the Ingredients between toasted tortillas and enjoy!

Roasted Asparagus with Hollandaise Sauce

Prep time: 10 minutes / Cook time: 10 minutes / Serves 4

Ingredients
- 400g asparagus spears, trimmed and cut into

2.5cm chunks
- 1 tbsp butter, melted
- 1 tsp cayenne pepper
- Sea salt and ground black pepper, to taste
- Hollandaise Sauce:
- 120g butter
- 2 egg yolks
- 1/2 tsp tarragon vinegar
- A squeeze of fresh lemon juice

Instructions
1. Toss the asparagus spears with 1 tablespoon of butter, cayenne pepper, salt, and black pepper; transfer them to the lightly-greased cooking basket.
2. Select zone 1 and pair it with "ROAST" at 200°C for 6 minutes. Select "MATCH" to duplicate settings across both zones. Press the "START/STOP" button.
3. Meanwhile, melt the butter in a saucepan; keep the butter warm.
4. Whisk the egg yolks, vinegar, and a splash of ice-cold water in a glass bowl that can fit over a saucepan. Put the bowl over the saucepan of barely simmering water. Whisk for about 4 minutes, until the sauce has thickened.
5. Remove from the heat and gradually whisk in the reserved butter. Add a squeeze of lemon juice and keep warm until ready to serve.
6. Place asparagus on serving plates and spoon over a generous helping of warm hollandaise sauce. Devour!

Cheesy Spicy Stuffed Mushrooms

Prep time: 10 minutes / Cook time: 10 minutes / Serves 4

Ingredients
- 8 large mushrooms, stems removed and chopped
- 1 tbsp butter
- 1/2 tsp chilli powder
- 1/2 tsp dried basil
- 1/2 tsp dried rosemary
- Sea salt and ground black pepper, to your liking
- 1 bell pepper, seeded and chopped
- 50g ricotta cheese, crumbled
- 2 tbsp breadcrumbs

Instructions
1. Insert crisper plates in both drawers. Spray crisper plates with nonstick cooking oil.
2. Pat the mushroom caps dry using tea towels.

3. In a mixing bowl, thoroughly combine the remaining Ingredients, including the reserved mushroom stems; divide the filling among the mushroom caps.
4. Select zone 1 and pair it with "ROAST" at 190°C for 10 minutes. Select "MATCH" to duplicate settings across both zones. Press the "START/STOP" button.
5. Bon appétit!

Vegan Kabobs Shish Kebabs

Prep time: 10 minutes / Cook time: 15 minutes / Serves 4

Ingredients
- 100g soy curls
- 100ml hot water
- 2 tbsp vegan BBQ sauce
- 1/2 tsp garlic granules
- Sea salt and ground black pepper, to taste
- 2 tsp olive oil
- 2 bell peppers, deseeded and chopped into large chunks
- 10 pearl onions
- 1 small aubergine, cut into cubes

Instructions
1. Soak soy curls in hot water for approximately 10 minutes. Drain the soy curls in a mesh sieve, squeezing out all excess liquid.
2. Toss the soy curls with BBQ sauce, garlic granules, salt, pepper, and 1 teaspoon of olive oil.
3. Toss the vegetables with the remaining 1 teaspoon of olive oil, salt, and pepper.
4. Add the soy curls to the zone 1 drawer and the vegetables to the zone 2 drawer.
5. Select zone 1 and pair it with "AIR FRY" at 180°C for 13 minutes. Select zone 2 and pair it with "ROAST" at 200°C for 15 minutes. Select "SYNC" followed by the "START/STOP" button.
6. When zone 1 time reaches 7 minutes, toss soy curls to ensure even browning. Reinsert the drawers to resume cooking.
7. When zone 2 time reaches 10 minutes, remove pearl onions from the basket. Reinsert the drawers to resume cooking.
8. Alternately thread the soy curls and vegetables onto the skewers until you run out of the Ingredients.
9. Bon appétit!

Vegan Carrot Dogs

Prep time: 1 hour / Cook time: 12 minutes / Serves 4

Ingredients
- 4 large carrots
- 1 tbsp soy sauce (or coconut aminos)
- 1 tsp apple cider vinegar
- 1 tsp smoked paprika
- 1 tsp English mustard powder
- 1 tbsp agave syrup
- 1 tsp garlic granules
- 1/2 teaspoon onion powder
- 1 tbsp olive oil
- 4 whole wheat hot dog buns

Instructions
1. Add all Ingredients, except the buns, to a ceramic (or glass) bowl; leave to marinate for about 1 hour.
2. Select zone 1 and pair it with "ROAST" at 180°C for 12 minutes. Select zone 2 and pair it with "BAKE" at 180°C for 5 minutes. Select "SYNC" followed by the "START/STOP" button.
3. Serve carrot dogs on whole wheat hot dog buns and add toppings of choice.
4. Bon appétit!

Roasted Rainbow Salad

Prep time: 10 minutes / Cook time: 15 minutes / Serves 4

Ingredients
- 200g acorn squash, peeled and cut into 1cm chunks
- 200g cauliflower florets
- 2 bell peppers, deseeded and cut into 1cm chunks
- 2 medium carrots, sliced
- Sea salt and ground black pepper, to taste
- 1 medium onion, quartered
- 1 small cucumber, sliced
- 1/2 tsp marjoram
- 1/2 tsp dried oregano
- 2 tbsp extra-virgin olive oil
- 1 tsp apple cider vinegar
- 1 teaspoon Dijon mustard

Instructions
1. Toss the squash, cauliflower, peppers, and carrots with salt and pepper until they are well coated.
2. Then, add the squash and cauliflower florets to the zone 1 drawer and peppers and carrots to the zone 2 drawer.

3. Select zone 1 and pair it with "ROAST" at 200°C for 12 minutes. Select zone 2 and pair it with "BAKE" at 200°C for 15 minutes. Select "SYNC" followed by the "START/STOP" button.
4. Add the remaining Ingredients to the bowl and toss to combine well. Serve at room temperature and enjoy!

Vegan Breakfast Sausage

Prep time: 10 minutes / Cook time: 20 minutes / Serves 4-5

Ingredients
- 240g can chickpea, drained
- 240g can red beans, drained
- 2 tbsp sunflower seeds
- 2 tsp sesame seeds
- 4 garlic cloves, peeled
- 1 medium onion, peeled and quartered
- 10g oat flour
- 1 tsp baking powder
- 1 tsp ground cumin
- 1/2 tsp dried basil
- Sea salt and freshly ground black pepper, to taste
- 1 tbsp olive oil

Instructions
1. Insert crisper plates in both drawers. Spray crisper plates with nonstick cooking oil.
2. In your blender or food processor, blend the Ingredients until everything is well incorporated.
3. Shape the mixture into patties and place them in the cooking basket.
4. Select zone 1 and pair it with "AIR FRY" at 180°C for 20 minutes. Select "MATCH" followed by the "START/STOP" button.
5. When zone 1 time reaches 10 minutes, turn them over using silicone-tipped tongs. Reinsert the drawers to continue cooking.
6. Bon appétit!

Traditional Caprese Sandwich

Prep time: 10 minutes / Cook time: 20 minutes / Serves 4

Ingredients
- 300g brown mushrooms, cut into larger chunks
- 2 large bell peppers, deseeded and sliced
- 2 tsp olive oil
- Sea salt and ground black pepper, to taste
- 1/2 tsp garlic granules
- 30g pesto
- A small handful of basil leaves
- 1 small red onion, sliced
- 2 tsp thick balsamic vinegar
- 1 large ciabatta, cut into four pieces

Instructions
1. Toss mushrooms and bell peppers with 1 teaspoon of olive oil, salt, black pepper, and garlic granules.
2. Place the mushrooms in the zone 1 drawer and the peppers in the zone 2 drawer.
3. Select zone 1 and pair it with "AIR FRY" at 180°C for 13 minutes. Select zone 2 and pair it with "ROAST" at 200°C for 15 minutes. Select "SYNC" followed by the "START/STOP" button.
4. At the halfway point, toss your food to promote even cooking; reinsert the drawer to resume cooking.
5. Drizzle the cut side of the bread with 1 teaspoon of olive oil and place them in the cooking basket. Bake at 190°C for 5 minutes, until they are toasted and lightly charred.
6. Assemble your sandwiches with all the Ingredients and enjoy!

CHAPTER 9 DESSERTS

Greek-Style Mug Cakes

Prep time: 5 minutes / Cook time: 10 minutes / Serves 4

Ingredients
- 200g chocolate chunks
- 2 tsp coconut oil
- 2 tbsp honey
- 4 tbsp Greek yoghurt
- 4 tbsp ground walnuts
- 4 tbsp self-raising flour

Instructions
1. Divide the Ingredients between four ramekins. Lower the ramekins into both drawers.
2. Select zone 1 and pair it with "BAKE" at 180°C for 10 minutes. Select "MATCH" followed by the "START/STOP" button.
3. Devour!

Fruit Crumble Muffins

Prep time: 10 minutes / Cook time: 30 minutes / Serves 8

Ingredients
- 120g unsalted butter, softened
- 120g golden caster sugar
- 1 tsp ground cinnamon
- 2 eggs
- 120g natural yoghurt
- 1 tsp vanilla extract
- 250g plain flour
- 1 tsp baking powder
- 1/2 tsp bicarbonate of soda
- A pinch of coarse salt
- 100g blueberries or blackberries
- 2 nectarines, stoned and cut into small pieces
- 1 tbsp demerara sugar

Instructions
1. Line 8 muffin cases with cupcake liners.
2. Beat 100g of the butter, caster sugar, and cinnamon with an electric whisk. Then, gradually fold in the eggs, yoghurt, and vanilla.
3. Combine 200g of flour with baking powder, bicarb, and salt. Divide 1/2 of the batter between muffin cases.

4. Gently push the fruits into the cases. Divide the rest of the batter between the cases, spooning it over the fruit.
5. Mix the remaining flour, butter, and demerara sugar with your fingers. Add a little of the crumble mixture to each muffin.
6. Select zone 1 and pair it with "BAKE" at 170°C for 30 minutes. Select "MATCH" followed by the "START/STOP" button.
7. Leave to cool in the tin for 10 minutes before serving. Bon appétit!

Fried Cinnamon Banana

Prep time: 10 minutes / Cook time: 13 minutes / Serves 6

Ingredients
- 3 ripe bananas, peeled and sliced lengthwise
- 2 tbsp agave nectar
- 1 tsp coconut oil
- 4 tbsp shredded coconut
- 1/4 tsp cardamom powder
- 1 tsp cinnamon powder

Instructions
1. Insert crisper plates in both drawers. Spray crisper plates with nonstick cooking oil.
2. Drizzle agave nectar, coconut oil, coconut, cardamom, and cinnamon over banana slices. Place banana slices on crisper plates.
3. Select zone 1 and pair it with "AIR FRY" at 190°C for 13 minutes. Select "MATCH" followed by the "START/STOP" button.
4. Bon appétit!

Roasted Cherries

Prep time: 10 minutes / Cook time: 20 minutes / Serves 6

Ingredients
- 200g dark sweet cherries
- 1 tbsp honey
- 1 tbsp rum
- 1/2 tsp vanilla

Instructions
1. Toss your cherries with the other Ingredients and

place them in the foil-lined cooking basket.

2. Select zone 1 and pair it with "ROAST" at 185°C for 20 minutes. Select "MATCH" followed by the "START/STOP" button.

3. Serve at room temperature and enjoy!

Grandma's Apple Fritters

Prep time: 10 minutes / Cook time: 13 minutes / Serves 6

Ingredients

- 100g cake flour
- 2 tbsp granulated sugar
- A pinch of sea salt
- 1 tsp baking powder
- 1 tsp cinnamon powder
- 1 large egg, whisked
- 100ml full-fat milk
- 1 large apple, peeled, cored & sliced into rings
- Powdered sugar, for garnish

Instructions

1. Mix the flour, sugar, salt, baking powder, and cinnamon.
2. In a separate bowl, whisk the egg with milk; add this wet mixture to dry Ingredients; mix to combine well.
3. Dip apple rings into the batter and transfer them to the foil-lined cooking basket.
4. Select zone 1 and pair it with "AIR FRY" at 185°C for 13 minutes. Select "MATCH" followed by the "START/STOP" button.
5. Serve with powdered sugar and enjoy!

Blackberry Tarts

Prep time: 30 minutes / Cook time: 13 minutes / Serves 6

Ingredients

- 150g blackberries, thinly sliced
- 1 tsp fresh lemon juice
- 1 tsp ginger powder
- 1 tbsp maple syrup
- 1 tbsp chia seeds
- 300g (7 ounces) box of refrigerated puff pastry
- 30g powdered sugar

Instructions

1. Cook blackberries over low heat until they start to get syrupy. Mash them and add the lemon juice, ginger powder, and maple syrup.
2. Remove from the heat and stir in the chia seeds. Let

the fruit mixture stand for approximately 30 minutes or until it has thickened.

3. Unroll the puff pastry and cut them into small rectangles. Spoon the berry mixture into the centre of each rectangle; top with another piece of the puff pastry.

4. Repeat until you run out of Ingredients. Brush mini tarts with nonstick oil and place them in both drawers.

5. Select zone 1 and pair it with "BAKE" at 175°C for 13 minutes. Select "MATCH" followed by the "START/STOP" button.

6. Dust with powdered sugar and enjoy!

Stuffed Apples and Pears

Prep time: 10 minutes / Cook time: 15 minutes / Serves 4

Ingredients

- 100g quick-cooking oats
- 50ml clear honey
- 100g walnuts, roughly chopped
- 1/4 tsp grated nutmeg
- 1 tsp cinnamon powder
- 2 medium apples, stems and seeds removed
- 2 medium pears, stems and seeds removed
- 4 tbsp coconut, shredded

Ingredients

1. In a mixing bowl, combine quick-cooking oats, honey, walnuts, nutmeg, and cinnamon.
2. Divide the filling mixture between your apples and pears. Lower the apples and pears into the lightly oiled cooking basket.
3. Select zone 1 and pair it with "BAKE" at 175°C for 15 minutes. Select "MATCH" followed by the "START/STOP" button.
4. Garnish with coconut shreds and enjoy!

Fruit Skewers

Prep time: 10 minutes / Cook time: 12 minutes / Serves 5

Ingredients

- 1 mango, cut into bite-sized chunks
- 1 medium pear, cut into bite-sized chunks
- 1 small pineapple, cut into bite-sized chunks
- 100g grapes
- 1/2 tsp cinnamon powder
- 1 tbsp fresh lime juice
- 1 tbsp maple syrup

Instructions

1. Toss all Ingredients in a mixing bowl. Tread fruit pieces on soaked bamboo skewers.
2. Lower the skewers into both drawers.
3. Select zone 1 and pair it with "AIR FRY" at 180°C for 12 minutes. Select "MATCH" followed by the "START/STOP" button.
4. Bon appétit!

Easy Molten Cakes

Prep time: 10 minutes / Cook time: 12 minutes / Serves 6

Ingredients

- 100g dark chocolate
- 100g butter, melted
- 1 large egg, whisked
- 50g brown sugar
- 30g oat flour
- 60g almond flour
- 1 tsp baking powder
- 1/4 tsp ground star anise
- 1/2 tsp ground cinnamon
- A pinch of grated nutmeg
- A pinch of sea salt

Instructions

1. Melt the chocolate and butter in a heatproof bowl. Mix the eggs with brown sugar until frothy.
2. Pour the chocolate mixture into the egg mixture. Stir in the remaining Ingredients. Using an electric hand whisk, mix until all the Ingredients are well incorporated.
3. Divide the mixture among the darioles and lower them into the cooking basket.
4. Select zone 1 and pair it with "BAKE" at 180°C for 12 minutes. Select "MATCH" followed by the "START/STOP" button. Devour!

Summer Peach and Apricot Crisp

Prep time: 10 minutes / Cook time: 33 minutes / Serves 6

Ingredients

- 2 large peaches, pitted and sliced
- 6 large apricots, pitted and quartered
- 50g golden caster sugar
- 1/2 tsp ground cinnamon
- 2 tbsp cornstarch
- Topping:
- 100g old-fashioned rolled oats
- 50g pecans, coarsely chopped
- 100g granulated sugar
- 1 tsp vanilla extract
- A pinch of salt
- 40ml coconut oil, melted

Instructions

1. Toss your peaches and apricot with golden caster sugar, cinnamon, and cornstarch. Place them in two lightly greased baking trays.
2. Put all the topping Ingredients in a bowl and rub together using your fingers until a crumb-like texture has formed.
3. Lowe the baking trays into the cooking basket.
4. Select zone 1 and pair it with "BAKE" at 165°C for 33 minutes. Select "MATCH" followed by the "START/STOP" button. Devour!

Individual Treacle Tarts

Prep time: 30 minutes / Cook time: 35 minutes / Serves 6

Ingredients

- 180g plain flour
- 75 butter, chilled
- 1 large egg
- Filling:
- 1 large egg yolk
- 250ml golden syrup, warmed
- 1/2 ball stem ginger in syrup, finely chopped
- 100g fine cookie crumbs
- 60 ml warmed treacle
- 1 tsp vanilla extract
- 1 tsp fresh lemon juice

Instructions

1. Mix the flour and butter until the mixture resembles crumbs. Fold in the egg and enough chilled water to form a ball; refrigerate the dough for about 30 minutes.
2. On a dry and clean work surface, roll out dough. Now, divide the dough into 6 equal pieces. Roll out thinly until the pastry is large enough to cover the base and sides of each tin.
3. Next, line shallow flan tins with pastry sheets; trim the edges and lower them into the cooking basket.
4. Select zone 1 and pair it with "BAKE" at 170°C for 35 minutes. Select "MATCH" followed by the "START/STOP" button.
5. Meanwhile, whisk all Ingredients for the filling.
6. At the half point, gently pour the filling mixture into

the flan tins. Reinsert the drawers to resume cooking and bake your tarts until set.

7. Bon appétit!

Spiced Roasted Pineapple

Prep time: 10 minutes / Cook time: 10 minutes / Serves 4

Ingredients
- 1 large pineapple, cut into rings
- 2 tbsp fresh orange juice
- 2 tbsp clear honey
- 1/2 tsp cinnamon powder
- 2 tbsp coconut, shredded

Instructions
1. Insert crisper plates in both drawers. Spray crisper plates with nonstick cooking oil.
2. Toss all Ingredients in a mixing bowl. Let them stand for about 10 minutes to absorb the flavours and release the juices. Lower the pineapple rings onto crisper plates.
3. Select zone 1 and pair it with "BAKE" at 190°C for 10 minutes. Select "MATCH" followed by the "START/STOP" button.
4. Turn them over halfway through the cooking time.
5. Dust with powdered sugar, if desired. Devour!

The Best Crème Brûlée Ever

Prep time: 10 minutes / Cook time: 22 minutes / Serves 4

Ingredients
- 250ml whipped cream
- 1 tsp vanilla essence
- 200ml milk
- 3 large eggs
- 200g granulated sugar
- Garnish:
- 2 tbsp brown sugar
- 4 tbsp berries of choice

Instructions
1. Whip the cream, vanilla, milk, and eggs in a saucepan.
2. Add granulated sugar to the pan and cook until the sugar has dissolved. Add the cream to the pan and remove it from the heat. Pour the mixture into ramekins.
3. Lower the ramekins into both drawers.
4. Select zone 1 and pair it with "BAKE" at 190°C for 20 minutes. Select "MATCH" followed by the

"START/STOP" button.

5. When ready to serve, sprinkle brown sugar and berries over the top. Then, caramelize the layer of sugar at 200°C for 2 minutes. Devour!

Vanilla Pancake Cake

Prep time: 5 minutes / Cook time: 10 minutes / Serves 4

Ingredients
- 50 g plain flour
- ½ tsp baking powder
- 40 g butter
- 1 egg
- ½ tsp vanilla extract
- ½ tsp cinnamon
- 30 g caster sugar

Instructions
1. Mix flour, sugar and baking powder in a bowl.
2. Add butter, egg, vanilla and cinnamon to the bowl.
3. Pour batter into a cake tin (of a size that will fit into your airfryer basket)
4. Cook in the airfryer at 160°C for 8 minutes.

Chocolate Chip Cookies

Prep time: 5 minutes / Cook time: 8 minutes / Serves 10 cookies

Ingredients
- 110 g plain flour
- 75 g butter
- 15 g white sugar
- 40 g brown sugar
- 1 egg
- 1 tsp vanilla extract
- 2 handfuls chocolate chips
- ½ tsp baking soda
- ¼ tsp sea salt

Instructions
1. Beat the brown and white sugar with the butter.
2. Add the egg and vanilla extract and beat well.
3. Add all the dry Ingredients and mix until combined.
4. Add chocolate chips and mix again.
5. Line airfryer basket with greaseproof paper.
6. Pierce holes in the greaseproof paper to allow air to circulate.
7. Form dough into balls.
8. Cook in the airfryer for about 8 minutes, allowing plenty of room between dough balls.